Mastering AutoGen

A Complete Guide to Automating Workflows with AI

©

Written By

Morgan Devline

Copyright

Mastering AutoGen: A Complete Guide to Automating Workflows with AI
© 2024 Morgan Devline
All rights reserved.

No part of this book may be reproduced, distributed, or transmitted in any form or by any means, including photocopying, recording, or other electronic or mechanical methods, without the prior written permission of the publisher, except in the case of brief quotations embodied in critical reviews and certain other non-commercial uses permitted by copyright law. For permission requests, write to the publisher at the address below.

Disclaimer
The information contained in this book is for educational and informational purposes only. The author and publisher make no representations or warranties with respect to the accuracy, applicability, or completeness of the contents of this book. The examples and case studies are for illustrative purposes and should not be construed as professional advice or endorsements. Readers are advised to seek professional consultation for specific applications.

The author and publisher shall not be liable for any loss or damages arising from the use of this book. All trademarks, product names, and company names or logos mentioned in this book are the property of their respective owners and are used for identification purposes only. Use of these names, logos, and brands does not imply endorsement.

Table of Content

Foreword 5
Part I: Understanding AutoGen and Its Foundations 9
Chapter 1: Introduction to AutoGen 10
Chapter 2: Getting Started with AutoGen 18
Chapter 3: Core Components of AutoGen Systems 26
Chapter 4: Ethical Considerations and Best Practices 35
Part II: Practical Applications of AutoGen 43
Chapter 5: Automating Content Generation 44
Chapter 6: Code Generation and Software Development 52
Chapter 7: Workflow Automation with Multi-Agent Systems 63
Chapter 8: Enhancing Customer Support 78
Chapter 9: Data Analysis and Report Generation 87
Chapter 10: Creative Ideation 102
Chapter 11: Decision Support Systems 111
Chapter 12: Knowledge Management 128
Chapter 13: Personalized Education and Training 139
Chapter 14: Prototyping and Simulation 150
Part III: Advanced Topics and Emerging Trends 160
Chapter 15: Integrating AutoGen with Emerging Technologies 161
Chapter 16: Scaling and Optimizing AutoGen Systems 172
Chapter 17: Security and Compliance in AutoGen 183
Chapter 18: Monitoring and Observability in AutoGen Systems .. 193
Chapter 19: Advanced AutoGen Techniques and Customizations 203
Part IV: Real-World Applications and Case Studies 213
Chapter 20: AutoGen in Healthcare 214
Chapter 21: AutoGen in Finance 223
Chapter 22: AutoGen in E-commerce 232

Chapter 23: AutoGen in Education 241

Chapter 24: AutoGen in Marketing and Advertising 251

Chapter 25: AutoGen in Manufacturing 259

Part V: Future Trends and Innovations in AutoGen 268

Chapter 26: Emerging Trends in AI-Driven Automation 269

Chapter 27: The Future of AutoGen 279

Part VI: Community, Resources, and Supplementary Materials .. 288

Chapter 28: Building and Leveraging the AutoGen Community .. 289

Chapter 29: Troubleshooting and Optimization Techniques 297

Chapter 30: Case Study Methodology 306

Chapter 31: Feedback Mechanisms and Continuous Improvement
.... 315

Appendix A: Glossary of Key Terms 323

Appendix B: Additional Resources and References 324

Appendix C: Sample AutoGen Workflows and Templates 326

Appendix D: Troubleshooting and FAQs 328

Appendix E: Contributor Bios 329

Index 330

Foreword

Acknowledgments

Creating a comprehensive guide like **"Mastering AutoGen: A Complete Guide to Automating Workflows with AI"** is a monumental task that requires the support and collaboration of many individuals and organizations. I would like to extend my deepest gratitude to all who have contributed to the development and completion of this book.

Firstly, my heartfelt thanks go to the team of experts in the field of artificial intelligence and automation who provided invaluable insights and feedback during the writing process. Your expertise ensured that the content is both accurate and relevant, bridging the gap between theoretical concepts and practical applications.

I am also grateful to the numerous beta readers who took the time to review early drafts of this book. Your constructive criticism and suggestions helped refine the material, making it more accessible and engaging for readers of all levels.

Special thanks to my family and friends for their unwavering support and encouragement. Your belief in my vision kept me motivated throughout the challenging phases of writing and publishing.

Lastly, I would like to acknowledge the contributions of the numerous open-source communities and developers whose tools and frameworks form the backbone of the AutoGen systems discussed in this book. Your dedication to advancing technology inspires the next generation of innovators.

About the Author

Morgan Devline is a seasoned software engineer and AI enthusiast with over a decade of experience in the tech industry. Holding a Master's degree in Computer Science from the prestigious Tech University, Morgan has dedicated his career to exploring the intersections of artificial intelligence, automation, and workflow optimization.

Throughout his professional journey, he has worked with leading technology firms, developing cutting-edge solutions that leverage AI to streamline complex processes. His expertise spans various domains, including machine learning, natural language processing, and multi-agent systems, making him a versatile contributor to the field of automation.

In addition to his industry accomplishments, Morgan is a passionate educator and mentor. He has conducted numerous workshops and seminars aimed at empowering professionals and enthusiasts to harness the power of AI in their respective fields. His commitment to knowledge sharing is evident in his previous publications and his active participation in technology forums and communities.

Morgan's vision for **"Mastering AutoGen"** stems from his belief in the transformative potential of AI-driven automation. He aims to provide readers with a thorough understanding of AutoGen systems, equipping them with the skills and knowledge necessary to implement effective automation strategies in diverse settings.

How to Use This Book

"Mastering AutoGen: A Complete Guide to Automating Workflows with AI" is designed to cater to a wide audience, ranging from beginners eager to delve into the world of AI automation to seasoned professionals seeking to enhance their existing workflows. To maximize the benefits of this book, it is essential to understand its structure and the supplementary materials available.

Navigating the Book's Structure

The book is meticulously organized into six main parts, each focusing on different aspects of AutoGen systems:

- **Part I: Understanding AutoGen and Its Foundations**
  Lays the groundwork by introducing fundamental concepts, setting up the necessary environments, and exploring core components of AutoGen systems.

- **Part II: Practical Applications of AutoGen**
  Delves into real-world applications across various industries, providing hands-on projects and case studies to illustrate practical implementations.

- **Part III: Advanced Topics and Emerging Trends**
  Explores sophisticated techniques, integration with emerging technologies, and future trends shaping the landscape of AI-driven automation.

- **Part IV: Real-World Applications and Case Studies**
  Presents detailed case studies from diverse sectors, highlighting successful AutoGen implementations and their impact.

- **Part V: Future Trends and Innovations in AutoGen**
  Discusses upcoming advancements and innovations, preparing readers for the evolving future of automation.

- **Part VI: Community, Resources, and Supplementary Materials**
  Focuses on building and leveraging the AutoGen community, troubleshooting techniques, and providing additional resources to support continuous learning.

Each chapter within these parts follows a consistent structure:

1. **Introduction**
   Provides an overview of the chapter's focus and objectives.

2. **Concepts and Techniques**
   Breaks down complex topics into understandable segments, supported by practical examples.

3. **Case Studies**
   Illustrates real-world applications and outcomes of the discussed concepts.

4. **Hands-On Project**
   Offers step-by-step guidance for implementing the chapter's lessons in a practical project.

5. **Practice Problems and Quizzes**
   Reinforces learning through exercises and adaptive quizzes designed to test comprehension and application skills.

6. **End-of-Chapter Summaries**
   Summarizes key takeaways and provides quick reference guides for easy revision.

By following this structured approach and utilizing the comprehensive resources provided, **"Mastering AutoGen: A Complete Guide to Automating Workflows with AI"** will equip you with the knowledge and tools necessary to harness the full potential of AI-driven automation in your professional endeavors.

Part I: Understanding AutoGen and Its Foundations

Chapter 1: Introduction to AutoGen

Automation and artificial intelligence (AI) are transforming the way individuals and organizations operate, enabling unprecedented levels of efficiency, creativity, and innovation. **AutoGen**, short for Automated Generative Systems, represents the convergence of **workflow automation** and **generative AI**, offering tools and techniques that allow for the automation of complex tasks, content creation, and decision-making processes. This chapter introduces AutoGen, exploring its definition, evolution, benefits, and key applications in modern industries.

1.1 What is AutoGen?

1.1.1 Definition and Scope

AutoGen refers to the integration of automation and generative AI systems designed to automate tasks, create content, and optimize workflows. By leveraging AI models capable of understanding and generating human-like text, images, code, and more, AutoGen systems extend beyond traditional automation, providing flexibility, intelligence, and creativity.

Key Characteristics of AutoGen:

1. **Automation of Repetitive Tasks:** Reduces manual effort in processes such as content generation, software development, and data analysis.

2. **Generative Capabilities:** Produces new outputs (e.g., text, code, visuals) based on predefined inputs and rules.

3. **Scalability:** Enables rapid execution of large-scale tasks with minimal human intervention.

4. **Integration with Existing Tools:** Works seamlessly with platforms like GitHub, Microsoft Office, and cloud services (AWS, Azure, Google Cloud).

Examples of AutoGen Applications:

- Generating blog posts and social media content.
- Automating customer support with chatbots.
- Refactoring and optimizing codebases.
- Enhancing decision-making with AI-driven insights.

Scope of AutoGen: AutoGen systems are applicable across diverse fields, including:

- **Marketing:** Content creation, ad campaigns, and personalized outreach.
- **Software Development:** Automating boilerplate code, testing, and deployment pipelines.
- **Design and Media:** Creating images, videos, and animations.
- **Education:** Generating lesson plans, quizzes, and personalized learning materials.
- **Business Operations:** Workflow orchestration, process optimization, and report generation.

1.1.2 Historical Evolution of Automation and Generative AI

Early Automation:

- **1950s-1970s:** The first wave of automation focused on manufacturing and industrial processes, with robots and assembly lines revolutionizing production.
- **1980s-1990s:** Software tools like Microsoft Excel and early databases enabled businesses to automate data entry, calculations, and reporting.

Introduction of AI:

- **1990s-2000s:** AI research advanced with machine learning techniques, enabling systems to learn from data. Early applications included spam filters and recommendation systems.

- **2010s:** The rise of deep learning led to breakthroughs in natural language processing (NLP) and computer vision. Key innovations included image recognition and voice assistants like Siri and Alexa.

Generative AI and Modern Automation:

- **2020s:** The introduction of transformer-based models, such as OpenAI's GPT series, enabled AI to generate human-like text, code, and visuals. AutoGen systems emerged as tools that combined automation with generative capabilities to address complex challenges.

1.2 Importance of Workflow Automation in the Modern Era

Workflow automation is essential for improving efficiency, reducing costs, and enabling organizations to focus on strategic initiatives. AutoGen elevates workflow automation by adding intelligence and adaptability to traditional systems.

1.2.1 Benefits and Return on Investment (ROI)

Key Benefits of AutoGen:

1. **Time Savings:** Automates repetitive tasks, freeing up time for higher-value activities.
    - **Example:** Generating personalized email campaigns for thousands of customers.

2. **Cost Reduction:** Minimizes labor costs by reducing manual effort.
    - **Example:** Automating code reviews instead of hiring additional developers.

3. **Enhanced Creativity:** Produces unique content and designs that would be labor-intensive for humans to create.
   - **Example:** Using AI to generate marketing visuals and slogans.

4. **Consistency and Accuracy:** Reduces errors in repetitive tasks, ensuring consistent quality.
   - **Example:** Automating data entry and report generation.

5. **Scalability:** Enables businesses to scale operations without proportional increases in resources.
   - **Example:** Automating customer service through AI chatbots.

ROI Considerations:

- **Implementation Costs:** Include software licensing, infrastructure setup, and training.
- **Operational Savings:** Measure reduced labor hours, improved efficiency, and higher output quality.
- **Long-Term Gains:** Focus on scalability, improved decision-making, and enhanced customer satisfaction.

ROI Formula:

$$ROI = \frac{Net\ Benefits\ (Savings - Costs)}{Implementation\ Costs} \times 100$$

Example ROI Calculation: A company automates its content creation process using AutoGen, saving 200 labor hours monthly. At an average rate of $50/hour, the savings amount to $10,000/month. With an implementation cost of $50,000, the ROI after six months is:

$$ROI = \frac{(60{,}000 - 50{,}000)}{50{,}000} \times 100 = 20\%$$

1.2.2 Impact on Industries and Job Roles

1. Impact on Industries:

- **Healthcare:** Automating patient data analysis, report generation, and appointment scheduling.
- **Finance:** Enhancing fraud detection, risk assessment, and personalized financial planning.
- **E-commerce:** Streamlining inventory management, personalized recommendations, and order tracking.

2. Impact on Job Roles: AutoGen changes job roles by shifting focus from manual tasks to strategic activities:

- **Marketing Professionals:** Transition from manual content creation to overseeing AI-driven campaigns.
- **Software Developers:** Focus on designing and improving AI-assisted tools rather than repetitive coding.
- **Customer Support Agents:** Manage complex queries while chatbots handle routine interactions.

Example: A customer support agent's role evolves from answering common questions to analyzing chatbot data and improving customer satisfaction strategies.

1.3 Overview of AutoGen Applications

AutoGen's versatility makes it a game-changer across multiple domains, offering solutions tailored to specific needs.

1.3.1 Summary of Key Use Cases

1. Content Creation:

- Generate articles, blogs, social media posts, and marketing copy.
- **Tools:** GPT-4, Jasper, Copy.ai.

- **Example:** A marketing team uses GPT-4 to create daily social media posts.

2. Software Development:
- Automate code generation, refactoring, and testing.
- **Tools:** GitHub Copilot, TabNine.
- **Example:** A developer uses Copilot to generate boilerplate code for a REST API.

3. Customer Support:
- Deploy chatbots for 24/7 customer service.
- **Tools:** ChatGPT, Zendesk AI.
- **Example:** An e-commerce site uses AI chatbots to handle FAQs and order tracking.

4. Design and Media:
- Create images, videos, and animations.
- **Tools:** DALL-E, MidJourney, Runway ML.
- **Example:** A designer uses DALL-E to generate concept art for a product launch.

5. Workflow Automation:
- Streamline processes like invoice management and data analysis.
- **Tools:** Zapier, Microsoft Power Automate.
- **Example:** A small business automates invoicing and payment reminders.

1.3.2 Future Prospects and Trends

1. Increased Adoption of AI-Driven Systems:
- Organizations will increasingly rely on AutoGen to enhance productivity and innovation.

2. Cross-Platform Integrations:

- AutoGen will integrate seamlessly with tools like CRM systems, cloud platforms, and IoT devices.

3. Ethical and Regulatory Considerations:

- As AutoGen grows, ethical AI practices and compliance with regulations (e.g., GDPR, CCPA) will become paramount.

4. Democratization of AI:

- Accessible tools and platforms will enable individuals and small businesses to leverage AutoGen capabilities.

Emerging Trends:

1. **Real-Time Collaboration:** AI systems that collaborate with teams in real time to enhance creativity and decision-making.
2. **Custom AI Models:** Domain-specific AutoGen systems tailored to unique business needs.
3. **AI-Augmented Creativity:** Enhanced tools for generating music, art, and interactive media.

Tables

AutoGen Feature	Example Use Case	Key Tools
Text Generation	Writing blogs and articles	GPT-4, Jasper
Image Creation	Designing marketing visuals	DALL-E, MidJourney
Code Automation	Generating boilerplate code	GitHub Copilot, TabNine
Workflow Orchestration	Automating data entry	Zapier, Power Automate
Customer Support	Chatbots for routine queries	ChatGPT, Zendesk AI

Figure 1.1: Historical Evolution of Automation

- Early Automation: Assembly lines in the 1950s.
- Rise of Machine Learning: Recommendation systems in the 2000s.
- Generative AI: GPT-3 and DALL-E in the 2020s.

AutoGen systems represent a paradigm shift in automation and generative AI, offering transformative solutions for content creation, software development, customer support, and beyond. By understanding the foundations, applications, and benefits of AutoGen, businesses and individuals can harness its potential to streamline workflows, enhance creativity, and achieve unprecedented levels of efficiency.

Chapter 2: Getting Started with AutoGen

This chapter provides a comprehensive guide to setting up your AutoGen environment, navigating popular platforms, running your first workflow, and mastering best practices for efficient implementation. By the end of this chapter, you'll have the foundational knowledge and tools to start leveraging AutoGen in your workflows.

2.1 Setting Up Your AutoGen Environment

2.1.1 Required Tools and Technologies

To get started with AutoGen, you'll need the following tools and technologies:

1. Hardware Requirements:

- **Minimum Requirements:**
    - Processor: Intel i5 or equivalent.
    - RAM: 8GB.
    - Storage: 10GB free space.

- **Recommended Requirements:**
    - Processor: Intel i7 or equivalent.
    - RAM: 16GB+.
    - GPU: NVIDIA GPU with CUDA support for accelerated AI tasks.

2. Software Requirements:

- **Operating System:**
    - Windows 10/11, macOS, or Linux (Ubuntu recommended).

- **Programming Language:**
    - Python 3.8 or later.
- **Libraries and Frameworks:**
    - Core Libraries: numpy, pandas, requests.
    - AutoGen Libraries: langchain, transformers.
- **Development Tools:**
    - IDE: VS Code, PyCharm, or Jupyter Notebook.
    - Version Control: Git and GitHub.

3. **Cloud and API Services:**
- **Cloud Providers:** AWS, Azure, or Google Cloud (optional for advanced use cases).
- **API Access:** OpenAI API key or other AutoGen service keys.

2.1.2 Installation Guides and Initial Configuration

Step-by-Step Installation:

1. **Install Python:**
    - Download Python from python.org.
    - Verify installation:

bash

```
python --version
```

2. **Set Up a Virtual Environment:**
    - Create and activate a virtual environment:

```bash
python -m venv autogen_env
source autogen_env/bin/activate  # For macOS/Linux
autogen_env\Scripts\activate    # For Windows
```

3. **Install Required Libraries:**
   - Install AutoGen-related packages:

```bash
pip install langchain transformers numpy pandas
```

4. **Configure API Access:**
   - Save your API key as an environment variable:

```bash
export OPENAI_API_KEY='your_api_key'  # macOS/Linux
set OPENAI_API_KEY=your_api_key       # Windows
```

5. **Verify Installation:**
   - Test the setup by running a simple script:

```python
from langchain.llms import OpenAI
llm = OpenAI(model="text-davinci-003", api_key="your_api_key")
print(llm("Hello, AutoGen!"))
```

2.2 Navigating AutoGen Platforms

2.2.1 Overview of Popular AutoGen Platforms

1. LangChain:

- **Purpose:** Simplifies the integration of LLMs into applications.
- **Key Features:**
  - Chainable workflows for advanced AI applications.
  - Built-in support for OpenAI and Hugging Face models.
- **Example Use Case:** Automating multi-step data analysis.

2. AutoGen Frameworks:
- **Purpose:** Provide modular solutions for AutoGen systems.
- **Key Features:**
  - Plug-and-play components for diverse tasks.
  - Workflow orchestration tools.

2.2.2 Comparative Analysis of Features and Capabilities

Feature	LangChain	AutoGen Frameworks
Ease of Use	Beginner-friendly	Moderate learning curve
Integration Support	Extensive	Limited but growing
Customizability	High	Moderate
Deployment Options	Local & Cloud	Cloud-focused

2.3 Running Your First AutoGen Workflow
2.3.1 Step-by-Step Tutorial

Objective: Create a simple text generator using LangChain.

Steps:

1. **Import Necessary Libraries:**

```python
from langchain.llms import OpenAI
```

2. **Initialize the Model:**

```python
llm = OpenAI(model="text-davinci-003", api_key="your_api_key")
```

3. **Generate Text:**

```python
prompt = "Write a short introduction about AutoGen."
response = llm(prompt)
print(response)
```

Expected Output:

```csharp
AutoGen is an innovative technology that integrates automation and generative AI...
```

2.3.2 Common Pitfalls and How to Avoid Them

1. API Key Errors:

- **Issue:** Invalid or missing API key.
- **Solution:** Double-check environment variables or configuration files.

2. Library Conflicts:

- **Issue:** Version mismatches.
- **Solution:** Use a virtual environment and pin library versions in requirements.txt.

3. **Slow Performance:**
   - **Issue:** Insufficient hardware.
   - **Solution:** Utilize cloud GPUs for intensive tasks.

2.4 Best Practices for Beginners

Tips for Efficient Learning and Implementation

1. **Start Small:** Focus on simple projects before tackling complex workflows.
2. **Use Pre-Built Tools:** Leverage existing libraries to save development time.
3. **Document Your Workflow:** Maintain clear documentation for reproducibility.

Resources for Continued Education

1. **Online Tutorials:**
   - LangChain documentation: LangChain Docs
   - OpenAI API guides: OpenAI API
2. **Community Forums:**
   - GitHub Discussions
   - AutoGen Subreddits and Discord channels

Books and Courses:
   - "Practical AI Automation" by industry experts.
   - Online courses on Coursera and Udemy.

2.5 Quick-Start Guides and Cheat Sheets
2.5.1 Essential Commands and Configurations

1. Common Commands:

- Install libraries:

bash

```
pip install <library_name>
```

- Activate virtual environment:

bash

```
source env/bin/activate
```

2. Configuration Tips:

- Save reusable API keys in .env files:

makefile

```
OPENAI_API_KEY=your_api_key
```

2.5.2 Quick Reference for Common Tasks

Task	Command/Code Snippet
Install LangChain	pip install langchain
Initialize LLM	llm = OpenAI(api_key="your_api_key")
Generate Text	response = llm("Your prompt here")
Set Environment Var	export OPENAI_API_KEY="your_api_key" (Linux/Mac)

By following the guidance in this chapter, you have set up your AutoGen environment, explored popular platforms, and successfully run your first workflow. With these foundations, you're ready to dive deeper into the practical applications and advanced features of AutoGen in the following chapters

Chapter 3: Core Components of AutoGen Systems

AutoGen systems rely on several key components to function effectively, from advanced machine learning models to integration frameworks. This chapter explores the foundational elements of AutoGen systems, providing a comprehensive understanding of their architecture, tools, and integration strategies. By grasping these components, readers can develop robust AutoGen workflows tailored to specific needs.

3.1 Large Language Models (LLMs)

Large Language Models (LLMs) form the backbone of many AutoGen systems, enabling tasks like text generation, summarization, and contextual understanding.

3.1.1 Architecture and Functionality

1. Core Concepts of LLMs:

- **Transformers Architecture:**
    - LLMs are built on transformer models, which use self-attention mechanisms to process input sequences in parallel.
    - Key Components:
        - **Encoder-Decoder:** Transforms input into meaningful representations and generates output.
        - **Self-Attention:** Captures contextual relationships within the data.
        - **Feedforward Layers:** Enhance processing power for deep learning tasks.

- **Training on Large Datasets:**
    - LLMs are pre-trained on diverse datasets (e.g., books, websites) and fine-tuned for specific applications.
- **Tokenization:**
    - Converts text into tokens (smaller pieces) for processing.
    - Example: Tokenizing "AutoGen is powerful" into [AutoGen, is, powerful].

2. Functional Capabilities of LLMs:

- Text generation, completion, and summarization.
- Code generation and debugging.
- Language translation and sentiment analysis.

Example Code Using OpenAI GPT:

python

```python
from langchain.llms import OpenAI

# Initialize the model
llm = OpenAI(model="text-davinci-003", api_key="your_api_key")

# Generate text
prompt = "Explain the core architecture of large language models."
response = llm(prompt)
print(response)
```

3.1.2 Leading Models (e.g., GPT-4, LLaMA 3)

1. GPT-4 (Generative Pre-trained Transformer 4):

- Developed by OpenAI.

- **Features:**
    - Generates human-like text.
    - Handles complex queries with enhanced reasoning.
    - Supports multiple languages.
- **Applications:**
    - Content creation, coding assistance, and virtual assistants.

2. **LLaMA 3 (Large Language Model Meta AI):**
- Developed by Meta AI.
- **Features:**
    - Optimized for efficiency and scalability.
    - Capable of running on resource-limited devices.
- **Applications:**
    - Real-time chatbots, personalized recommendations, and lightweight AI solutions.

Feature	GPT-4	LLaMA 3
Model Size	Large-scale	Smaller, efficient
Language Support	Multilingual	Multilingual
Use Cases	General-purpose	Lightweight applications

3.2 Multi-Agent Systems

Multi-agent systems are a vital component of AutoGen, enabling collaborative problem-solving and task delegation among AI agents.

3.2.1 Concepts and Interactions

1. Definition:

- Multi-agent systems consist of multiple autonomous entities (agents) that interact, communicate, and collaborate to achieve a shared goal.

2. Key Concepts:

- **Autonomy:** Each agent can make decisions independently.
- **Coordination:** Agents work together to optimize tasks.
- **Communication:** Agents share information through predefined protocols.

Example:

- In a customer service scenario, one agent handles FAQ responses while another processes refund requests.

3.2.2 Designing Collaborative Agents

1. Steps to Design Collaborative Agents:

- Define agent roles and responsibilities.
- Implement communication protocols (e.g., HTTP, WebSockets).
- Develop decision-making algorithms for task delegation.

2. Code Example of Collaborative Agents:

python
```
class Agent:
    def __init__(self, name, task):
        self.name = name
        self.task = task
```

```python
    def execute_task(self):
        return f"{self.name} is executing {self.task}"

# Create agents
agent1 = Agent("FAQ Agent", "Answer FAQs")
agent2 = Agent("Refund Agent", "Process Refunds")

# Collaboration
print(agent1.execute_task())
print(agent2.execute_task())
```

3.3 Integration with APIs and Existing Software

APIs enable seamless interaction between AutoGen systems and external applications, making integration a cornerstone of AutoGen workflows.

3.3.1 RESTful APIs and Webhooks

1. RESTful APIs:

- Allow communication between systems using standard HTTP methods (GET, POST, PUT, DELETE).

- **Example:**
    - Fetching data from an external service:

python

```
import requests

url = "https://api.example.com/data"
response = requests.get(url)
print(response.json())
```

2. Webhooks:

- Facilitate event-driven communication by sending data to a specified endpoint when an event occurs.
- **Example Use Case:**
    - Notifying a server when a new customer signs up.

3.3.2 Middleware and Integration Platforms

1. Middleware:

- Acts as a bridge between different systems to enable seamless communication.
- Examples: Apache Kafka, RabbitMQ.

2. Integration Platforms:

- Tools like Zapier and Microsoft Power Automate simplify integration by offering pre-built connectors.

3.4 Data Pipelines and Workflow Orchestration

Managing and automating data flow is essential for effective AutoGen workflows.

3.4.1 ETL Processes

1. Definition:

- ETL (Extract, Transform, Load) processes involve:
    - **Extracting** data from sources.
    - **Transforming** it into a usable format.
    - **Loading** it into a target system.

2. Example Workflow:

python

import pandas as pd

# Extract
data = pd.read_csv("data.csv")

Transform
data["processed_column"] = data["raw_column"].apply(lambda x: x * 2)

# Load
data.to_csv("processed_data.csv", index=False)

3.4.2 Automation Tools and Frameworks

Popular Tools:

- Apache Airflow: For orchestrating workflows.
- Prefect: Simplifies ETL automation with Python.

3.5 Platform-Specific Integrations

Tailoring AutoGen systems to specific platforms enhances functionality and scalability.

3.5.1 Integrating with AWS, Azure, and Google Cloud

1. AWS Integration:

- Use AWS Lambda for serverless automation.
- **Example:**

python

```python
import boto3

s3 = boto3.client("s3")
s3.upload_file("file.txt", "bucket-name", "file.txt")
```

2. Azure Integration:

- Utilize Azure Logic Apps for workflow automation.

3. Google Cloud Integration:

- Implement Google Cloud Functions for lightweight automation tasks.

3.5.2 Cross-Platform Automation Techniques

1. Use Containers:

- Deploy applications using Docker for portability.

2. Unified Interfaces:

- Leverage APIs and SDKs to ensure consistent cross-platform operations.

Example:

- Integrating an application with both AWS S3 and Google Cloud Storage.

This chapter outlined the core components of AutoGen systems, from LLMs and multi-agent systems to APIs and data pipelines. Understanding these foundational elements equips you with the knowledge to design, implement, and optimize robust AutoGen workflows in diverse environments. The next chapter will explore ethical considerations and best practices for deploying AutoGen systems responsibly.

Chapter 4: Ethical Considerations and Best Practices

The rapid growth of automation and generative AI, including AutoGen systems, presents both transformative opportunities and significant challenges. Ethical considerations are paramount to ensuring these technologies are deployed responsibly, safely, and inclusively. This chapter explores key ethical issues, including data privacy, bias, sustainability, and societal impact, while providing actionable guidelines and case studies to address these concerns effectively.

4.1 Data Privacy and Security

Data privacy and security are critical when implementing AutoGen systems, especially as they often handle sensitive information such as customer data, personal details, and intellectual property.

4.1.1 Protecting Sensitive Information

1. Principles of Data Protection:

- **Minimization:** Only collect and process the data necessary for the task.
- **Anonymization:** Remove personally identifiable information (PII) where possible.
- **Encryption:** Use encryption to secure data at rest and in transit.

2. Strategies for Securing Data:

- **Role-Based Access Control (RBAC):**
    - Limit data access based on user roles.
    - Example:

```yaml
- role: admin
  permissions: ["read", "write", "delete"]
- role: user
  permissions: ["read"]
```

- **Regular Audits:**
    - Conduct periodic security audits to identify and address vulnerabilities.
- **Secure APIs:**
    - Use authentication tokens and HTTPS to secure API communications.

3. Example of Data Encryption:

```python
from cryptography.fernet import Fernet

# Generate a key
key = Fernet.generate_key()
cipher_suite = Fernet(key)

# Encrypt data
data = "Sensitive Information"
encrypted_data = cipher_suite.encrypt(data.encode())
print("Encrypted:", encrypted_data)

# Decrypt data
decrypted_data = cipher_suite.decrypt(encrypted_data).decode()
print("Decrypted:", decrypted_data)
```

4.1.2 Compliance with Regulations (e.g., GDPR, CCPA)

1. **Key Regulations:**
   - **GDPR (General Data Protection Regulation):**
     - Requires businesses to protect EU citizens' data privacy.
     - **Rights Covered:** Right to access, rectify, and erase personal data.
   - **CCPA (California Consumer Privacy Act):**
     - Empowers California residents to control their personal information.

2. **Ensuring Compliance:**
   - Implement a transparent privacy policy.
   - Allow users to opt-out of data collection.
   - Maintain data processing logs for auditing purposes.

Example Compliance Policy:

json

```
{
  "privacy_policy": {
    "data_collected": ["Name", "Email", "Browsing History"],
    "usage": "Improving user experience",
    "user_rights": ["Access", "Delete"]
  }
}
```

4.2 Mitigating Bias in AI Models

Bias in AI systems can perpetuate inequality, reduce fairness, and erode trust. Addressing bias is essential for ensuring inclusivity and fairness.

4.2.1 Identifying and Addressing Bias

1. Sources of Bias:

- **Data Bias:** Training datasets that underrepresent certain groups.
- **Algorithm Bias:** Flawed algorithms amplifying stereotypes.

2. Methods to Identify Bias:

- **Diversity Audits:** Analyze datasets for representation gaps.
- **Performance Metrics:** Evaluate AI performance across demographic groups.

3. Strategies to Address Bias:

- Augment datasets with diverse samples.
- Regularly retrain models on updated, balanced data.

4.2.2 Ensuring Fairness and Inclusivity

1. Fairness Metrics:

- **Equal Opportunity:** Ensure similar outcomes for different demographic groups.
- **Calibration:** Align predicted probabilities with observed outcomes.

2. Implementation Example:

python

```
from sklearn.metrics import classification_report

# Evaluate model performance
y_true = [1, 0, 1, 1, 0]  # Ground truth labels
y_pred = [1, 0, 1, 0, 0]  # Model predictions
```

```
report = classification_report(y_true, y_pred, target_names=["Group A", "Group B"])
print(report)
```

4.3 Sustainable and Responsible AI Usage

Sustainability is a growing concern in AI deployment, as training and running large models consume significant resources.

4.3.1 Environmental Impact

1. Energy Consumption:

- Training a single large-scale AI model can emit as much carbon as five cars over their lifetimes.

2. Strategies for Mitigation:

- Use energy-efficient hardware (e.g., GPUs optimized for AI).
- Choose cloud providers with renewable energy commitments.

4.3.2 Long-Term Sustainability Strategies

1. Optimize Model Efficiency:

- Use smaller, task-specific models when possible (e.g., GPT-4 fine-tuning).

2. Implement Green AI Practices:

- **Example:** Monitor and reduce energy usage with tools like CodeCarbon.

python

```
from codecarbon import EmissionsTracker

tracker = EmissionsTracker()
```

```
tracker.start()

# Code to run AI task
result = sum([i**2 for i in range(100000)])

tracker.stop()
```

4.4 Ethical Decision-Making Frameworks

Deploying AutoGen systems ethically requires clear guidelines and frameworks to navigate complex dilemmas.

Guidelines for Ethical AI Deployment

Transparency: Clearly explain how the system operates. 2. **Accountability:** Assign responsibility for AI decisions. 3. **Continuous Monitoring:** Regularly evaluate AI systems for unintended consequences.

Case Studies on Ethical Dilemmas

1. **Case Study: Biased Recruitment Tool**

   - A recruitment AI favored certain demographics due to biased training data.
   - **Resolution:** Retrained the model with diverse data and implemented fairness audits.

4.5 Deep Dive into Ethical AI and Societal Impact

4.5.1 Balancing Automation with Human Employment

1. **Challenges:**

- Risk of job displacement in repetitive tasks.
- Growing demand for upskilling.

2. Strategies:
- Focus on augmentation rather than replacement.
- Invest in training programs for affected workers.

4.5.2 Strategies for Mitigating Negative Effects

1. Promote Inclusive AI Development:
- Involve diverse teams in AI design and testing.

2. Support Affected Communities:
- Create programs to support workers transitioning to new roles.

4.6 Best Practices Checklist

4.6.1 Summarized Guidelines for Responsible AutoGen Implementation

1. Data Privacy and Security:
- Encrypt sensitive information.
- Comply with legal regulations (e.g., GDPR, CCPA).

2. Mitigating Bias:
- Regularly audit datasets for fairness.
- Evaluate model performance across demographics.

3. Sustainable Practices:
- Optimize workflows for energy efficiency.
- Select green cloud providers.

4. Ethical Deployment:

- Maintain transparency and accountability.
- Develop ethical guidelines tailored to your industry.

Ethical considerations are a cornerstone of deploying AutoGen systems responsibly. By adhering to the principles of data privacy, fairness, sustainability, and transparency, organizations can harness the transformative power of AutoGen while minimizing risks and ensuring societal benefits. This chapter provided actionable guidelines and case studies to navigate the ethical complexities of AutoGen, setting a foundation for responsible innovation.

Part II: Practical Applications of AutoGen

Chapter 5: Automating Content Generation

Automation in content creation has revolutionized industries such as marketing, journalism, and design. With advancements in AI, particularly AutoGen systems, it is now possible to generate high-quality text, images, and videos at scale. This chapter provides an in-depth exploration of content generation tools, use cases, and practical applications, offering hands-on guidance and ready-to-use templates for leveraging AutoGen in real-world scenarios.

5.1 Text Generation

Text generation refers to the automated creation of coherent and meaningful text using AI-powered tools and models.

5.1.1 Tools and Techniques

1. Tools for Text Generation:

- **OpenAI GPT:** Versatile and powerful language model for generating text, summarizing, and answering questions.
- **Jasper:** AI writing assistant focused on marketing and creative content.
- **Copy.ai:** Specialized in short-form content like social media posts and ad copy.

2. Techniques for Effective Text Generation:

- **Fine-Tuning Models:** Customize models with domain-specific data for specialized outputs.
- **Prompt Engineering:** Crafting detailed and precise prompts to guide the AI.

Example of Prompt Engineering:

python

```python
from langchain.llms import OpenAI

llm = OpenAI(model="text-davinci-003", api_key="your_api_key")
prompt = """
Write a 150-word blog introduction for a post titled 'The Benefits of Workflow Automation.'
"""
response = llm(prompt)
print(response)
```

Expected Output:

kotlin

In today's fast-paced business environment, efficiency is the cornerstone of success. Workflow automation enables organizations to streamline repetitive tasks, reduce errors, and free up valuable resources for strategic decision-making. In this blog, we'll explore the top benefits of workflow automation and how it can revolutionize the way businesses operate.

5.1.2 Use Cases: Articles, Blogs, Marketing Copy

1. Articles and Blogs:

- Automating the drafting process for long-form content.
- **Example:** Writing technical blogs for a SaaS company.

2. Marketing Copy:

- Generating ad headlines, product descriptions, and email subject lines.

- **Example:** Creating a series of Instagram captions for a product launch.

Sample Output:

- **Input Prompt:** "Generate an email subject line promoting a 50% off sale."
- **AI Output:** "☐ Limited Time: Get 50% Off Your Favorite Products Today!"

5.2 Image and Video Generation

The ability to generate visuals using AI has transformed creative industries, enabling rapid prototyping, unique designs, and cost-efficient content production.

5.2.1 AI Models for Visual Content

1. DALL-E:

- Developed by OpenAI, DALL-E generates high-quality images from text prompts.
- **Example Prompt:** "Create an illustration of a futuristic cityscape at sunset."

2. MidJourney:

- Known for producing artistic and surreal visuals.
- **Example Prompt:** "A fantastical forest with glowing mushrooms and floating orbs."

3. Runway ML:

- Focuses on video generation and editing.

5.2.2 Applications in Design and Media

1. Design Applications:

- Automating the creation of logos, banners, and product mockups.

2. Media Applications:

- Generating storyboards and visual effects for films.

Example Code for DALL-E Integration:

python

```
import openai

openai.api_key = "your_api_key"

response = openai.Image.create(
    prompt="A serene beach with a futuristic robot walking along the shore",
    n=1,
    size="1024x1024"
)
image_url = response['data'][0]['url']
print(image_url)
```

5.3 Case Studies

5.3.1 Automating Blog Writing for a Tech Company

Scenario: A tech company needed weekly blogs on emerging AI trends. Using GPT-4 and fine-tuned data, they automated 80% of the content creation process, reducing costs by 40% and increasing publication frequency.

5.3.2 Personalized Email Campaigns for E-commerce

Scenario: An e-commerce store used AutoGen systems to create personalized email campaigns based on customer purchase history. The result was a 25% increase in click-through rates.

5.4 Hands-On Project

5.4.1 Building a Content Generator Bot from Scratch

Objective: Create a Python-based bot that generates text and images for social media campaigns.

Steps:

1. **Set Up Environment:**
   - Install necessary libraries:

bash

```
pip install openai pillow requests
```

2. **Generate Text:**

python

```
import openai

openai.api_key = "your_api_key"

prompt = "Write a tweet promoting eco-friendly travel."
response = openai.Completion.create(
    engine="text-davinci-003",
    prompt=prompt,
    max_tokens=50
)
print(response['choices'][0]['text'])
```

3. **Generate Image:**

python

```
response = openai.Image.create(
    prompt="An illustration of an electric car on a mountain road",
    n=1,
    size="512x512"
)
print(response['data'][0]['url'])
```

4. **Combine Outputs for Posting:**
    o Use the generated text and image URL to create a cohesive social media post.

5.5 Practice Problems and Quizzes

5.5.1 Reinforcing Key Concepts and Techniques

1. Practice Problem: Generate a list of five email subject lines for a fictional sale on winter clothing.

2. Solution:

plaintext

1. "❄ ☐ Stay Warm: Winter Sale Up to 50% Off!"

2. "☐ Winter Essentials at Unbeatable Prices!"

3. "Your Cozy Winter Wardrobe Awaits!"

4. "Don't Miss Out: Exclusive Winter Deals!"

5. "Limited Time: Bundle Up and Save Big!"

5.5.2 Interactive Quizzes: Adaptive Quizzes

Question: What is the primary benefit of prompt engineering in text generation?

1. Reduces API costs.
2. Ensures more accurate and relevant outputs.
3. Increases processing speed.

Answer: 2. Ensures more accurate and relevant outputs.

5.6 End-of-Chapter Summaries

5.6.1 Key Takeaways

- AutoGen enables rapid creation of text, images, and videos, revolutionizing content workflows.
- Tools like GPT-4, DALL-E, and Jasper streamline creative processes.

5.6.2 Quick Reference Guides

- **Text Generation:** Focus on detailed prompts for specific results.
- **Image Generation:** Use models like DALL-E for high-quality visuals.

5.7 Templates and Tools

5.7.1 Workflow Templates

Example Template for Blog Automation:

plaintext

1. Generate Outline: AI generates the blog's structure.
2. Expand Sections: Each section is expanded with AI.
3. Edit and Refine: Human review for accuracy and tone.
4. Publish: Final blog is scheduled or posted.

5.7.2 Scripts and Snippets

Reusable Snippet for Text Summarization:

python

```python
def summarize_text(api_key, text, max_length=50):
    import openai
    openai.api_key = api_key
    response = openai.Completion.create(
        engine="text-davinci-003",
        prompt=f"Summarize this: {text}",
        max_tokens=max_length
    )
    return response['choices'][0]['text']
```

Automating content generation is a transformative capability of AutoGen systems. From text and image generation to personalized campaigns, the applications are vast and impactful. This chapter provided tools, techniques, and hands-on examples to help you harness AutoGen for creative and professional content creation.

Chapter 6: Code Generation and Software Development

Modern software development increasingly relies on automation to streamline processes, improve efficiency, and enhance code quality. **AutoGen** systems play a pivotal role in transforming software engineering by automating repetitive tasks, refactoring code, and integrating AI-powered tools into development workflows. This chapter delves into the applications of AutoGen in code generation and software development, offering a detailed exploration of tools, techniques, case studies, and practical implementations.

6.1 Automating Boilerplate Code Creation

Boilerplate code refers to the repetitive and standardized sections of code often required in software projects, such as setting up classes, creating templates, or initializing configurations. Automating these tasks saves developers time and reduces the potential for human error.

6.1.1 Tools: GitHub Copilot, TabNine

1. GitHub Copilot:

- **Description:** Developed by GitHub in collaboration with OpenAI, Copilot acts as an AI-powered pair programmer, offering suggestions and generating boilerplate code within integrated development environments (IDEs).

- **Key Features:**
    - Autocompletes lines or blocks of code based on context.
    - Suggests implementations for functions or classes.
    - Supports multiple programming languages, including Python, JavaScript, Java, and more.

- **Example Use Case:**

- Generating a REST API endpoint in Python:

```python
# Prompt: Create a Flask endpoint to retrieve user data
from flask import Flask, jsonify, request

app = Flask(__name__)

@app.route('/users/<int:user_id>', methods=['GET'])
def get_user(user_id):
    # Mock user data
    user_data = {"id": user_id, "name": "John Doe", "email": "johndoe@example.com"}
    return jsonify(user_data)

if __name__ == '__main__':
    app.run(debug=True)
```

2. **TabNine:**
   - **Description:** An AI-powered code completion tool that integrates seamlessly with IDEs, offering contextual code suggestions.
   - **Key Features:**
     - Works offline for privacy-sensitive projects.
     - Provides language-agnostic support for various programming languages.
     - Integrates with popular IDEs such as VS Code, IntelliJ IDEA, and PyCharm.
   - **Example Use Case:**
     - Completing boilerplate code for a Java class:

```java
```

```java
// Prompt: Define a User class with id, name, and email attributes
public class User {
    private int id;
    private String name;
    private String email;

    public User(int id, String name, String email) {
        this.id = id;
        this.name = name;
        this.email = email;
    }

    // Getters and setters
    public int getId() {
        return id;
    }

    public void setId(int id) {
        this.id = id;
    }

    public String getName() {
        return name;
    }

    public void setName(String name) {
        this.name = name;
    }

    public String getEmail() {
        return email;
    }
```

```
public void setEmail(String email) {
    this.email = email;
  }
}
```

6.1.2 Best Practices for Efficient Coding

1. **Leverage AI Tools:**
   - Use GitHub Copilot, TabNine, or similar tools to automate repetitive coding tasks.
   - Regularly update these tools to ensure access to the latest features.

2. **Template Utilization:**
   - Create and use templates for common coding patterns (e.g., MVC, API endpoints, database connections).

3. **Code Reviews:**
   - Validate AI-generated code through peer reviews to ensure accuracy and maintain coding standards.

4. **Maintain Documentation:**
   - Document boilerplate code templates and workflows to facilitate consistency across projects.

6.2 Code Refactoring and Optimization

Refactoring involves restructuring existing code to improve its readability, maintainability, and efficiency without altering its external behavior. AutoGen systems assist in identifying suboptimal code patterns and automating the refactoring process.

6.2.1 Techniques for Improving Code Quality

1. **Simplifying Complex Logic:**
   - Break down long functions into smaller, reusable components.

- Example: Refactoring nested loops into modular functions.

2. **Improving Readability:**
    - Use descriptive variable and function names.
    - Format code consistently using tools like Prettier or Black.

3. **Eliminating Redundancies:**
    - Identify and remove duplicate code using static analysis tools.
    - Example: Merging repeated database queries into a single reusable function.

4. **Optimizing Performance:**
    - Replace inefficient algorithms with optimized alternatives.
    - Example: Using list comprehensions in Python instead of traditional loops.

6.2.2 Automated Code Reviews and Testing

1. Automated Code Reviews:

- Tools like **SonarQube** and **Codacy** analyze codebases to detect potential issues, including:
    - Code smells (e.g., overly complex methods).
    - Security vulnerabilities (e.g., SQL injection risks).
    - Deprecated or inefficient APIs.

2. Automated Testing:

- Implement unit tests, integration tests, and regression tests using tools such as:
    - **JUnit** (Java), **Pytest** (Python), or **Mocha** (JavaScript).

- Example: Automating unit tests in Python:

python

```
import unittest

def add(a, b):
    return a + b

class TestMathOperations(unittest.TestCase):
    def test_add(self):
        self.assertEqual(add(2, 3), 5)
        self.assertEqual(add(-1, 1), 0)

if __name__ == '__main__':
    unittest.main()
```

6.3 Integrating AutoGen in Development Environments

AI-powered tools integrate seamlessly into development environments, enhancing workflows and automating routine tasks.

6.3.1 Setting Up AI Assistants in IDEs

1. **Installation:**
    - Install extensions like GitHub Copilot or TabNine via the IDE marketplace.
    - Configure API keys or licensing information as required.

2. **Customization:**
    - Adjust settings to match your coding style and project requirements (e.g., enabling specific language support).

3. **Usage:**
   - Activate AI suggestions by typing or placing the cursor where code completion is needed.
   - Accept or modify suggestions based on context.

6.3.2 Workflow Automation with CI/CD Pipelines

1. **Continuous Integration (CI):**
   - Automate code building, testing, and merging using tools like **Jenkins, GitLab CI/CD**, or **CircleCI**.

2. **Continuous Deployment (CD):**
   - Deploy code changes automatically to production or staging environments.
   - Example: Using GitHub Actions to automate CI/CD workflows:

```yaml
name: CI/CD Pipeline

on:
  push:
    branches:
      - main

jobs:
  build-and-deploy:
    runs-on: ubuntu-latest
```

```yaml
steps:
  - name: Checkout Code
    uses: actions/checkout@v2

  - name: Set up Python
    uses: actions/setup-python@v2
    with:
      python-version: 3.8

  - name: Install Dependencies
    run: pip install -r requirements.txt

  - name: Run Tests
    run: pytest

  - name: Deploy
    run: echo "Deployment step here"
```

6.4 Case Studies

6.4.1 Streamlining Feature Development in a Web Application

Scenario: A development team needed to implement a new user authentication feature. By leveraging GitHub Copilot, they automated the generation of boilerplate code for user login, registration, and password recovery functionalities, saving significant time.

6.4.2 Reducing Bug Rates through Automated Testing

Scenario: A software company integrated automated testing tools like Pytest into their CI/CD pipelines, reducing bug occurrence by 35% and enhancing code reliability.

6.5 Hands-On Project
6.5.1 Developing an AI-Powered Code Refactoring Tool

Objective: Build a Python-based tool that uses AI to analyze and refactor code for better readability and efficiency.

6.6 Practice Problems and Quizzes
6.6.1 Practice Problem:

Refactor the following code to improve efficiency and readability:

python

```
numbers = [1, 2, 3, 4, 5]
squares = []
for num in numbers:
    squares.append(num ** 2)
```

Solution:

python

```
numbers = [1, 2, 3, 4, 5]
squares = [num ** 2 for num in numbers]
```

6.7 End-of-Chapter Summaries
6.7.1 Key Takeaways

- Tools like GitHub Copilot and TabNine simplify code generation.
- Automated testing and code reviews enhance quality and reliability.

6.8 Templates and Tools
Snippet 6.1: Template for Refactoring

python

```python
def refactor_code(input_code):
    # AI-powered logic for identifying issues and refactoring
    pass
```

This comprehensive chapter equips you with the tools and knowledge to integrate AutoGen into your software development workflows, boosting productivity and code quality.

Chapter 7: Workflow Automation with Multi-Agent Systems

Multi-agent systems (MAS) provide an innovative approach to workflow automation by leveraging the capabilities of multiple intelligent agents that work collaboratively to achieve complex goals. These systems are particularly useful in handling tasks requiring coordination, adaptability, and scalability. This chapter explores the fundamentals of MAS, effective workflow design, tools and frameworks, and real-world applications.

7.1 Fundamentals of Multi-Agent Systems

Multi-agent systems consist of independent agents that communicate, coordinate, and collaborate to perform tasks efficiently.

7.1.1 Agent Communication Protocols

Effective communication is critical for the success of MAS. Agents must share data, delegate tasks, and synchronize efforts.

1. **Types of Communication:**

    - **Direct Communication:**
        - Agents exchange information directly using structured protocols such as REST APIs or WebSockets.
        - **Example:**
            - An agent sends task updates to another via an API call.
            - Example API Request:

```json
{
  "sender": "Agent1",
  "recipient": "Agent2",
  "message": "Task completed successfully."
}
```

- **Brokered Communication:**
    - Agents communicate through a central broker or message queue, such as RabbitMQ or Kafka.
    - **Benefits:** Ensures message reliability and supports asynchronous communication.

2. **Communication Standards:**

- **FIPA (Foundation for Intelligent Physical Agents):**
    - Specifies standard communication protocols for agent interaction.
    - Example: Request-Response dialogues.
- **Message Passing Interfaces:**
    - Use of JSON, XML, or custom data serialization formats to ensure compatibility.

7.1.2 Coordination and Collaboration Strategies

Coordination and collaboration ensure that agents in a system work cohesively without conflicts.

1. **Coordination Models:**

- **Centralized Coordination:**
    - A central agent manages task distribution and monitors progress.

- - **Example:** A master agent allocates subtasks to worker agents.
- **Decentralized Coordination:**
  - Agents independently negotiate and delegate tasks.
  - **Example:** Peer-to-peer networks for load balancing.

2. Collaboration Techniques:

- **Shared Goals:**
  - All agents are programmed to prioritize system-wide objectives.
  - Example: A team of customer support agents working to reduce response times.
- **Dynamic Role Assignment:**
  - Agents dynamically assume roles based on system needs.
  - Example: An idle agent takes over a task from an overloaded peer.

7.2 Designing Effective Agent Workflows

Designing effective workflows involves careful planning to optimize task allocation, scalability, and system flexibility.

7.2.1 Task Allocation and Management

1. Task Allocation Strategies:

- **Static Allocation:**
  - Predefined task assignments for each agent.
  - **Example:** Agent A always handles customer queries, while Agent B processes refunds.
- **Dynamic Allocation:**

- Tasks are assigned based on real-time system states, such as workload or agent availability.
- Example:

python

```
def allocate_task(agent_pool, task):
    available_agent = next(agent for agent in agent_pool if agent.is_idle())
    available_agent.assign_task(task)
```

2. Task Prioritization:

- Implementing priority queues to ensure high-priority tasks are addressed first.
- Example: Processing urgent customer complaints before routine queries.

3. Monitoring and Feedback:

- Continuously monitor agent performance and task progress to ensure quality.
- Example: Logging agent activity:

python

```
log = {"agent": "Agent1", "task": "Generate Report", "status": "In Progress"}
print(log)
```

7.2.2 Ensuring Scalability and Flexibility

1. Horizontal Scaling:

- Adding more agents to handle increasing workloads.
- Example: Deploying additional virtual agents during peak hours.

2. Workflow Adaptability:

- Designing workflows that adapt to changing conditions or unexpected failures.
- Example: Reassigning tasks if an agent becomes unavailable.

7.3 Tools and Frameworks for Multi-Agent Systems

Selecting the right tools and frameworks is essential for building and managing efficient MAS workflows.

7.3.1 LangChain, AutoGen Platforms

1. LangChain:

- **Purpose:** Simplifies the integration of large language models (LLMs) into multi-agent workflows.
- **Features:**
    - Chainable workflows.
    - Built-in support for dialogue-based agents.
- **Example Use Case:** Coordinating agents for customer support automation.

2. AutoGen Platforms:

- **Purpose:** Provides pre-built frameworks for developing MAS workflows.
- **Features:**
    - Agent role definitions.
    - Task orchestration and monitoring.
- **Example Use Case:** Automating literature reviews with multiple research agents.

7.3.2 Comparative Analysis of Leading Tools

Feature	LangChain	AutoGen Platforms
Ease of Use	Beginner-friendly	Moderate
Integration Options	Extensive (APIs, cloud)	Limited to specific frameworks
Scalability	High	Moderate
Customization	High	Pre-defined components

7.4 Case Studies

7.4.1 Research Assistants for Literature Summarization

Scenario: A university research team used MAS to automate literature reviews. Each agent focused on a specific topic, summarized findings, and compiled a comprehensive report.

Workflow:

1. **Agent Roles:**
    - Agent 1: Search and retrieve articles.
    - Agent 2: Summarize article content.
    - Agent 3: Organize summaries into a cohesive report.

Code Example:

python

```python
class ResearchAgent:
    def __init__(self, role):
        self.role = role

    def perform_task(self, input_data):
        if self.role == "search":
            return f"Searching for {input_data}"
```

```
    elif self.role == "summarize":
        return f"Summarizing content: {input_data}"
    elif self.role == "organize":
        return f"Compiling summaries: {input_data}"

# Create agents
search_agent = ResearchAgent("search")
summarize_agent = ResearchAgent("summarize")
organize_agent = ResearchAgent("organize")

# Simulate workflow
articles = search_agent.perform_task("AI ethics")
summary = summarize_agent.perform_task(articles)
final_report = organize_agent.perform_task(summary)

print(final_report)
```

7.4.2 IT Troubleshooting Bots for Enterprise Systems

Scenario: An enterprise IT department implemented MAS to handle troubleshooting requests. Each agent specialized in specific tasks such as diagnostics, patching, and reporting.

Workflow:

1. **Agent Roles:**
    - Diagnostic Agent: Identifies issues.
    - Patching Agent: Applies fixes.
    - Reporting Agent: Logs resolution details.

Benefits:

- Reduced downtime by 50%.
- Improved accuracy and consistency in troubleshooting.

Workflow automation with multi-agent systems offers unparalleled efficiency, flexibility, and scalability. By leveraging tools like LangChain and AutoGen platforms, organizations can create intelligent systems capable of handling complex tasks collaboratively. This chapter has provided a comprehensive guide to understanding, designing, and implementing MAS workflows, illustrated with practical examples and real-world applications. The next chapter will delve deeper into advanced AutoGen applications, including decision support and knowledge management.

7.5 Hands-On Project

7.5.1 Creating a Multi-Agent AutoGen Pipeline for Data Processing

This hands-on project guides you through the creation of a **multi-agent AutoGen pipeline** designed for data processing tasks, such as cleaning, analyzing, and reporting. The project will demonstrate how agents can collaborate efficiently to automate workflows, providing you with a practical understanding of multi-agent systems.

Project Objective: Build a multi-agent system where:

1. **Data Extraction Agent** fetches raw data.
2. **Data Cleaning Agent** processes and cleans the data.
3. **Data Analysis Agent** generates insights from the cleaned data.
4. **Reporting Agent** formats the results into a report.

Step-by-Step Instructions:

1. Set Up Your Environment:
- Install necessary libraries:

bash

pip install pandas langchain

2. Define Agent Classes:
- Create classes for each agent with specific roles.

Code Example:

python

```python
import pandas as pd

class DataExtractionAgent:
    def fetch_data(self, source):
        print(f"Fetching data from {source}...")
        # Simulated raw data
        data = {"Name": ["Alice", "Bob", None], "Age": [25, None, 30], "Salary": [50000, 60000, None]}
        return pd.DataFrame(data)

class DataCleaningAgent:
    def clean_data(self, raw_data):
        print("Cleaning data...")
        cleaned_data = raw_data.dropna()  # Remove rows with missing values
        return cleaned_data

class DataAnalysisAgent:
    def analyze_data(self, cleaned_data):
        print("Analyzing data...")
        summary = cleaned_data.describe()
        return summary

class ReportingAgent:
```

```python
    def generate_report(self, analysis):
        print("Generating report...")
        report = f"Data Analysis Summary:\n{analysis}"
        return report
```

3. Implement the Workflow:

- Create instances of agents and define their interactions.

Code Example:

python

```python
# Instantiate agents
extraction_agent = DataExtractionAgent()
cleaning_agent = DataCleaningAgent()
analysis_agent = DataAnalysisAgent()
reporting_agent = ReportingAgent()

# Workflow
raw_data = extraction_agent.fetch_data("Database XYZ")
cleaned_data = cleaning_agent.clean_data(raw_data)
analysis = analysis_agent.analyze_data(cleaned_data)
report = reporting_agent.generate_report(analysis)

print("\nFinal Report:\n")
print(report)
```

4. Test the Workflow:

- Run the script and verify the outputs at each stage.

Expected Output:

plaintext

Fetching data from Database XYZ...

Cleaning data...

Analyzing data...

Generating report...

Final Report:

Data Analysis Summary:

	Age	Salary
count	2.000000	2.000000
mean	27.500000	55000.000000
std	3.535534	7071.067812
min	25.000000	50000.000000
max	30.000000	60000.000000

5. Enhance the Pipeline:

- Add error handling, logging, and visualization for a more robust system.

7.6 Practice Problems and Quizzes
7.6.1 Deepening Knowledge of Multi-Agent Coordination
Problem 1: Task Allocation

- **Scenario:** You are designing a multi-agent system for processing customer orders. The system includes:
    - **Order Validation Agent**
    - **Inventory Check Agent**
    - **Shipping Agent**
- **Task:** Define how tasks should flow between agents and implement a Python class structure to simulate this workflow.

Problem 2: Debugging Communication

- An agent fails to receive a task from another due to a missing API key. Identify potential fixes and write a script to validate API keys before communication.

7.6.2 Interactive Quizzes: Adaptive Quizzes

Quiz Example: Question 1: What is the primary purpose of a broker in multi-agent communication?

1. Directly manage task execution.
2. Facilitate reliable and asynchronous message passing.
3. Monitor agent performance.

Correct Answer: 2. Facilitate reliable and asynchronous message passing.

Question 2: Which coordination model is best for dynamic and distributed workflows?

1. Centralized coordination
2. Decentralized coordination
3. Task-agnostic coordination

Correct Answer: 2. Decentralized coordination

7.7 End-of-Chapter Summaries
7.7.1 Key Takeaways

- Multi-agent systems enable intelligent, collaborative workflows.
- Effective agent communication and coordination are critical for success.

- Tools like LangChain and AutoGen platforms simplify MAS development.

7.7.2 Quick Reference Guides

- **Agent Communication:** Use brokered communication for scalability.
- **Task Allocation:** Implement dynamic allocation for flexibility.
- **Tools:** Compare LangChain for advanced workflows vs. AutoGen platforms for ease of use.

7.8 Templates and Tools

7.8.1 Workflow Templates

Template 1: Multi-Agent Workflow for Content Generation

plaintext

1. Idea Generator Agent: Suggests blog topics.

2. Draft Writer Agent: Writes the initial draft.

3. Editor Agent: Refines and polishes the content.

4. Publisher Agent: Uploads the final content to the CMS.

7.8.2 Scripts and Snippets

Reusable Snippet for Task Monitoring:

python

```
class Agent:
    def __init__(self, name):
        self.name = name
        self.status = "Idle"
```

```python
    def assign_task(self, task):
        self.status = f"Working on {task}"
        print(f"{self.name}: {self.status}")

    def complete_task(self):
        print(f"{self.name}: Task completed.")
        self.status = "Idle"

# Example Usage
agent = Agent("DataProcessingAgent")
agent.assign_task("Clean Dataset")
agent.complete_task()
```

This chapter explored the practical applications of multi-agent systems, guiding readers through their fundamentals, workflow design, tools, and real-world use cases. The hands-on project and additional resources equip you with the knowledge and tools to implement your own multi-agent pipelines. Whether for data processing, IT troubleshooting, or creative content generation, MAS offers limitless possibilities for workflow automation.

Chapter 8: Enhancing Customer Support

Customer support is a critical touchpoint for any business, directly influencing customer satisfaction, retention, and brand loyalty. AutoGen systems enable the automation of various customer support tasks, including real-time chat, email responses, and knowledge base management. This chapter dives into AI-driven solutions for customer support, exploring their implementation, benefits, and practical applications.

8.1 Deploying AI-Powered Chatbots

AI-powered chatbots use natural language processing (NLP) and machine learning to engage with customers, answer queries, and provide support in real time.

8.1.1 Natural Language Understanding (NLU) and Dialogue Management

1. Understanding NLU:

- Natural Language Understanding (NLU) enables chatbots to interpret user input by:
    - Identifying **intents** (user's goal).
    - Extracting **entities** (specific details in the input).

Example:

- Input: "What's the status of my order #12345?"
    - **Intent:** Order Inquiry
    - **Entity:** Order #12345

2. Dialogue Management:

- The chatbot decides how to respond based on user input and context.
- Dialogue management tools like **Rasa** or **Dialogflow** handle:
    - Context tracking.
    - Multi-turn conversations.
    - Error handling.

Code Example (Using Rasa):

```yaml
intents:
  - greet
  - order_status

responses:
  utter_greet:
    - text: "Hello! How can I help you today?"
  utter_order_status:
    - text: "Please provide your order number."

stories:
  - story: Order inquiry
    steps:
      - intent: order_status
      - action: utter_order_status
```

8.1.2 Integrating with CRM Systems

1. Why Integrate with CRM?

- CRM integration allows chatbots to:
    - Access customer profiles and interaction history.

- Provide personalized responses.
- Log conversations for future analysis.

2. Steps for Integration:
1. **Connect CRM API:**
   - Example: Salesforce, HubSpot.
2. **Authentication:**
   - Use API keys or OAuth.
3. **Query CRM Data:**
   - Fetch customer details or update records.

Code Example (Connecting to a CRM API):

```python
import requests

crm_api_url = "https://api.crmplatform.com/customer"
headers = {"Authorization": "Bearer your_api_token"}

response = requests.get(f"{crm_api_url}/12345", headers=headers)
customer_data = response.json()
print(f"Customer Name: {customer_data['name']}")
```

8.2 Automated Email Responders

Automated email responders enhance efficiency by addressing common queries, personalizing responses, and escalating issues when necessary.

8.2.1 Personalization Techniques

1. Leveraging AI for Personalization:

- Use AI to analyze customer data and craft tailored email responses.
- Example: Mentioning customer-specific details like recent purchases.

2. Template-Based Personalization:

- Dynamically insert data into email templates.
- **Example Template:**

plaintext

Hello {customer_name},

Thank you for reaching out regarding {issue_topic}. We have escalated your concern and will update you by {resolution_date}.

Best regards,

The Support Team

Code Example:

python

```
template = "Hello {customer_name},\n\nThank you for reaching out regarding {issue_topic}."
personalized_email = template.format(customer_name="Alice", issue_topic="order delay")
print(personalized_email)
```

8.2.2 Managing Escalations with AI

1. **Identifying Escalation Triggers:**
   - Keywords like "angry," "escalate," or high sentiment negativity.

2. **Automated Escalation Process:**
   - Detect escalation needs using sentiment analysis.
   - Forward the email to a human agent or manager.

Example Workflow:

python

```python
from textblob import TextBlob

email_content = "I am very unhappy with the delay in my order!"
sentiment = TextBlob(email_content).sentiment.polarity

if sentiment < -0.5:
    print("Escalating to manager...")
else:
    print("Responding with a standard template.")
```

8.3 Building Dynamic Knowledge Bases

A dynamic knowledge base provides customers and agents with accurate and up-to-date information for solving problems efficiently.

8.3.1 Knowledge Graphs and Information Retrieval

1. **What are Knowledge Graphs?**
   - A structured way to represent and retrieve information.
   - Nodes represent entities; edges represent relationships.

2. **Example Knowledge Graph:**

- Nodes: Product A, Feature X, Issue Y.
- Edges: "Product A has Feature X," "Feature X causes Issue Y."

Code Example (Using NetworkX):

```python
import networkx as nx

graph = nx.DiGraph()
graph.add_edge("Product A", "Feature X", relation="has")
graph.add_edge("Feature X", "Issue Y", relation="causes")

print(nx.shortest_path(graph, "Product A", "Issue Y"))
```

8.3.2 Continuous Learning and Updates

1. AI-Driven Updates:

- Use AI to analyze customer interactions and update the knowledge base automatically.

2. Example: Adding New FAQs:

```python
def add_to_knowledge_base(question, answer, knowledge_base):
    knowledge_base[question] = answer
    return knowledge_base

kb = {}
kb = add_to_knowledge_base("What is AutoGen?", "AutoGen automates workflows.", kb)
print(kb)
```

8.4 Case Studies

8.4.1 Automating FAQs for a SaaS Company

Scenario: A SaaS company reduced its support workload by 60% by deploying an FAQ chatbot that retrieved answers from a dynamic knowledge base.

8.4.2 Handling Customer Inquiries at Scale for an E-commerce Platform

Scenario: An e-commerce platform implemented AI-powered email responders and chatbots, reducing response times by 50% during peak seasons.

8.5 Hands-On Project
8.5.1 Developing an AI-Powered Customer Support Agent

Objective: Create a chatbot that handles customer queries about product details and order statuses.

Steps:

1. **Define Intents:**
    - Order status, product details, greetings.
2. **Train a Model:**
    - Use Rasa or Dialogflow.
3. **Integrate with a CRM System:**
    - Fetch customer details based on query.

8.6 Practice Problems and Quizzes

8.6.1 Applying Customer Support Automation Techniques

Problem: Design a workflow for a chatbot that escalates issues after three failed attempts to resolve them.

8.6.2 Interactive Quizzes

Question: Which technique is most effective for personalization in email automation?

1. Static templates
2. AI-driven sentiment analysis
3. Dynamic data insertion

Answer: 3. Dynamic data insertion

8.7 End-of-Chapter Summaries

8.7.1 Key Takeaways

- AI-powered chatbots and email responders enhance efficiency and customer satisfaction.
- Knowledge bases are essential for scalable, accurate customer support.

8.7.2 Quick Reference Guides

- **NLU Tools:** Rasa, Dialogflow.
- **Personalization Techniques:** Dynamic templates, CRM integration.

This chapter explored how AutoGen systems can transform customer support through chatbots, email automation, and dynamic knowledge bases. By implementing these tools and techniques, businesses can improve response times, reduce costs, and enhance customer satisfaction.

Chapter 9: Data Analysis and Report Generation

Data analysis and report generation are critical for transforming raw information into actionable insights. Automation in these areas enhances efficiency, reduces manual effort, and enables real-time decision-making. This chapter explores tools, techniques, and practical applications of AutoGen systems for automating data collection, cleaning, interpretation, and visualization.

9.1 Automating Data Collection and Cleaning

Effective data analysis begins with collecting and preparing clean, consistent, and accurate data.

9.1.1 Tools and Techniques for ETL Processes

ETL Overview:

- **Extract:** Gather raw data from various sources (databases, APIs, files).
- **Transform:** Process and clean data to make it usable.
- **Load:** Store the cleaned data in a database or data warehouse.

Popular Tools:

- **Apache Airflow:** Orchestrates complex workflows.
- **Pandas:** Simplifies data manipulation in Python.
- **Talend:** A no-code/low-code platform for ETL processes.

Example ETL Workflow Using Python:

python

```
import pandas as pd

# Step 1: Extract data
data = pd.read_csv("raw_data.csv")

# Step 2: Transform data
data.dropna(inplace=True)  # Remove missing values
data['Sales'] = data['Sales'].apply(lambda x: x * 1.1)  # Apply transformation

# Step 3: Load data
data.to_csv("cleaned_data.csv", index=False)
print("ETL process completed successfully!")
```

Key Best Practices:

1. Automate repetitive steps with scripts or pipelines.
2. Validate data during extraction to avoid processing errors.
3. Document transformations for reproducibility.

9.1.2 Ensuring Data Quality and Consistency

Challenges:

- Missing values.
- Duplicate entries.
- Inconsistent formats.

Strategies to Ensure Quality:

1. **Validation:** Implement checks for data formats and ranges.
2. **Deduplication:** Remove duplicate entries using unique identifiers.

3. **Standardization:** Normalize data formats (e.g., dates, currencies).

Code Example for Data Quality Checks:

python

```
# Check for missing values
missing_values = data.isnull().sum()
print(f"Missing values:\n{missing_values}")

# Remove duplicates
data = data.drop_duplicates()
print("Duplicates removed.")

# Validate data ranges
if not (data['Age'] > 0).all():
    print("Invalid age detected.")
```

9.2 Generating Insights and Summaries

After preparing data, the next step is extracting insights and creating meaningful summaries.

9.2.1 Leveraging LLMs for Data Interpretation

Large Language Models (LLMs) like GPT-4 can assist in interpreting and summarizing datasets.

Use Cases:

- Generate natural language summaries of data trends.
- Provide recommendations based on insights.

Example Using LLM for Summary Generation:

python

```python
from langchain.llms import OpenAI

# Initialize the LLM
llm = OpenAI(model="text-davinci-003", api_key="your_api_key")

# Prompt to analyze data
prompt = """
Analyze the following data:
{'Sales': [500, 600, 550, 700], 'Region': ['East', 'West', 'East', 'West']}
Provide a summary of sales performance by region.
"""
response = llm(prompt)
print(response)
```

Expected Output:

vbnet

The West region outperformed the East region in total sales, with 1300 units compared to 1050 units.

9.2.2 Visualizing Data with AI Tools

AI tools like AutoGen systems can automatically generate data visualizations that are both insightful and aesthetically appealing.

Tools:

- **Matplotlib/Seaborn:** For static Python-based visualizations.
- **Plotly/Dash:** For interactive visualizations.

Example Visualization with Seaborn:

```python
import seaborn as sns
import matplotlib.pyplot as plt

# Sample data
data = pd.DataFrame({
    'Region': ['East', 'West', 'North', 'South'],
    'Sales': [500, 700, 400, 600]
})

# Bar chart
sns.barplot(x='Region', y='Sales', data=data)
plt.title("Sales by Region")
plt.show()
```

9.3 Integrating AutoGen with Data Visualization Libraries

AutoGen systems can interface with popular data visualization tools, enabling dynamic dashboards and presentations.

9.3.1 Tools: Tableau, PowerBI, D3.js

1. Tableau:

- Drag-and-drop interface for creating interactive dashboards.
- Integration with Python through Tableau's TabPy API.

2. Power BI:

- Microsoft's data visualization tool with seamless integration into Office 365.
- Supports Python and R for advanced customization.

3. D3.js:

- A JavaScript library for creating web-based, interactive visualizations.

Code Example: Exporting Data for Tableau:

python

```
data.to_csv("tableau_input.csv", index=False)
print("Data exported for Tableau visualization.")
```

9.3.2 Creating Interactive Dashboards

AutoGen can dynamically update dashboards using real-time data streams and APIs.

Example Dashboard with Plotly Dash:

python

```
import dash
from dash import html, dcc
import pandas as pd
import plotly.express as px

# Load data
data = pd.DataFrame({
    'Region': ['East', 'West', 'North', 'South'],
    'Sales': [500, 700, 400, 600]
})

# Create a Dash app
app = dash.Dash(__name__)
fig = px.bar(data, x='Region', y='Sales', title='Sales by Region')

app.layout = html.Div([
    html.H1("Sales Dashboard"),
```

```
    dcc.Graph(figure=fig)
])

if __name__ == '__main__':
    app.run_server(debug=True)
```

9.4 Case Studies

9.4.1 Building a Data Analytics Dashboard for a Financial Firm

Scenario: A financial firm used AutoGen systems to automate the creation of real-time dashboards tracking investment performance.

Key Features:

- Integration with live market data feeds.
- Automated generation of performance summaries.

Outcome:

- Reduced report generation time by 60%.
- Improved client engagement with interactive visuals.

9.4.2 Automating Market Research Reports for a Marketing Agency

Scenario: A marketing agency deployed AutoGen to automate competitor analysis and market trend reports.

Workflow:

1. Extract data from public sources.
2. Analyze trends using LLMs.
3. Generate PDF reports.

Outcome:

- Saved 40 hours per week on manual research.
- Increased report accuracy and consistency.

9.5 Hands-On Project
9.5.1 Developing an AI-Driven Data Analytics Platform

This hands-on project will guide you through the creation of an AI-powered data analytics platform. The platform will collect, clean, analyze, and visualize data using AutoGen systems and Python-based tools. By the end of the project, you'll have a functional prototype that can be extended for real-world applications.

Objective: Build a data analytics platform that:

1. Automates data collection and cleaning.
2. Generates insights using AI.
3. Creates interactive visualizations for better decision-making.

Step-by-Step Instructions:

Step 1: Set Up the Environment

1. Install Required Libraries:

bash

```
pip install pandas plotly dash openai
```

2. Ensure API keys for LLM (e.g., OpenAI) are available.

Step 2: Design the Workflow

1. **Data Collection:**

- Fetch data from a CSV file, API, or database.

2. **Data Cleaning:**
    - Remove missing or invalid entries.

3. **Data Analysis:**
    - Use AI to generate insights and trends.

4. **Visualization:**
    - Display data in interactive charts and dashboards.

Step 3: Implement the Platform

Code Implementation:

1. Data Collection and Cleaning:

python

```python
import pandas as pd

# Step 1: Load raw data
def load_data(file_path):
    return pd.read_csv(file_path)

# Step 2: Clean data
def clean_data(data):
    data.dropna(inplace=True)  # Remove rows with missing values
    data = data[data['Sales'] > 0]  # Remove invalid sales data
    return data

# Example usage
raw_data = load_data("sales_data.csv")
cleaned_data = clean_data(raw_data)
print(cleaned_data.head())
```

2. Data Analysis with AI:

python

```python
import openai

openai.api_key = "your_openai_api_key"

# Generate insights using GPT
def generate_insights(data):
    summary_prompt = f"Summarize the following sales data:\n{data.describe()}"
    response = openai.Completion.create(
        engine="text-davinci-003",
        prompt=summary_prompt,
        max_tokens=150
    )
    return response.choices[0].text

# Example usage
insights = generate_insights(cleaned_data)
print("Insights:\n", insights)
```

3. Data Visualization:

python

```python
import plotly.express as px

def create_visualization(data):
    fig = px.bar(data, x="Region", y="Sales", title="Sales by Region")
    fig.show()

# Example usage
create_visualization(cleaned_data)
```

4. Combine Workflow into a Dash Web App:

python

```
import dash
from dash import html, dcc

# Initialize Dash app
app = dash.Dash(__name__)

# Create the layout
app.layout = html.Div([
    html.H1("AI-Driven Data Analytics Platform"),
    dcc.Graph(figure=px.bar(cleaned_data, x="Region", y="Sales", title="Sales by Region")),
    html.H3("Insights"),
    html.Div(insights)
])

if __name__ == "__main__":
    app.run_server(debug=True)
```

Expected Output:

- A dynamic dashboard showing a bar chart of sales by region.
- AI-generated insights displayed below the chart.

9.6 Practice Problems and Quizzes

9.6.1 Enhancing Data Analysis Skills with AutoGen

Problem 1:

- **Task:** Write a function to detect outliers in the sales data using the IQR method.

Solution:

python

```
def detect_outliers(data, column):
    Q1 = data[column].quantile(0.25)
    Q3 = data[column].quantile(0.75)
    IQR = Q3 - Q1
    lower_bound = Q1 - 1.5 * IQR
    upper_bound = Q3 + 1.5 * IQR
    return data[(data[column] < lower_bound) | (data[column] > upper_bound)]

# Example usage
outliers = detect_outliers(cleaned_data, "Sales")
print("Outliers:\n", outliers)
```

Problem 2:

- **Task:** Create a pipeline to automate ETL and generate a summary report using LLM.

9.6.2 Interactive Quizzes: Adaptive Quizzes

Question 1: What is the primary benefit of using AI for data analysis?

1. Faster data cleaning.
2. Personalized insights generation.
3. Automated error handling.

Answer: 2. Personalized insights generation.

Question 2: Which library is best suited for creating interactive dashboards in Python?

1. Matplotlib
2. Plotly Dash

3. Seaborn

Answer: 2. Plotly Dash.

9.7 End-of-Chapter Summaries

9.7.1 Key Takeaways

- Automating data analysis involves ETL processes, AI-powered insights, and interactive dashboards.
- Tools like Pandas, Plotly, and OpenAI streamline workflows for analytics and reporting.
- Dynamic visualizations and AI summaries enhance decision-making.

9.7.2 Quick Reference Guides

Task	Tool/Library	Key Functionality
Data Cleaning	Pandas	Handle missing and inconsistent data.
Insights Generation	OpenAI GPT	Summarize and interpret data trends.
Visualization	Plotly Dash	Create interactive dashboards.

9.8 Templates and Tools

9.8.1 Workflow Templates

Template for AI-Driven Data Analytics Workflow:

1. **Step 1:** Extract data from multiple sources.
2. **Step 2:** Clean and preprocess data.
3. **Step 3:** Generate insights with LLMs.

4. **Step 4:** Visualize data in an interactive dashboard.
5. **Step 5:** Export results to a report or API.

9.8.2 Scripts and Snippets

Reusable Script for Real-Time Data Analysis:

python

```
def real_time_analysis(data_stream, llm):
    for data in data_stream:
        cleaned_data = clean_data(data)
        insights = generate_insights(cleaned_data)
        create_visualization(cleaned_data)
        print("Insights:\n", insights)
```

Exporting Data for Reporting:

python

```
def export_to_csv(data, filename="output.csv"):
    data.to_csv(filename, index=False)
    print(f"Data exported to {filename}")

# Example usage
export_to_csv(cleaned_data)
```

This chapter explored the automation of data analysis and report generation with AutoGen systems. By combining AI tools, ETL workflows, and visualization libraries, you can create scalable solutions for generating actionable insights. With hands-on projects, reusable templates, and practical tools, this chapter equips you to develop AI-driven analytics platforms for diverse applications.

Chapter 10: Creative Ideation

Creativity and innovation are at the heart of many industries, including art, design, storytelling, and marketing. With advancements in AI, tools like AutoGen systems are becoming essential in supporting creative processes. This chapter explores how AI assists in graphic design, storytelling, idea generation, and more, providing practical applications, case studies, and a hands-on project for readers to experiment with AI in creativity.

10.1 Supporting Innovation in Art and Design

AI has transformed the creative industry by introducing tools that can generate, enhance, and refine visual content, offering designers and artists new possibilities for innovation.

10.1.1 AI Tools for Graphic Design and Multimedia

1. Popular AI Tools:

- **Canva:** Provides AI-powered design suggestions and templates.
- **Runway ML:** Offers tools for video editing, style transfer, and content creation.
- **DALL-E:** Generates images from textual descriptions.

2. Applications in Graphic Design:

- Logo creation, banner design, and product mockups.
- Automating repetitive tasks like resizing and formatting.

Code Example for Using DALL-E:

python

```python
import openai

openai.api_key = "your_api_key"

response = openai.Image.create(
    prompt="A futuristic cityscape at sunset, digital art",
    n=1,
    size="1024x1024"
)
image_url = response['data'][0]['url']
print(f"Generated image URL: {image_url}")
```

10.1.2 Generative Adversarial Networks (GANs) in Creativity

1. Understanding GANs:

- GANs consist of two neural networks (generator and discriminator) that work together to create realistic content.
- **Use Cases:**
    - Creating realistic faces, landscapes, and textures.
    - Style transfer for applying artistic effects to photos.

2. Example Workflow Using GANs:

- **Input:** A sketch or description.
- **Output:** A fully rendered image or artwork.

Popular Tools:

- **StyleGAN:** Generates high-quality images.
- **DeepArt.io:** Transfers artistic styles to existing images.

Code Example Using StyleGAN:

python

```
# Assuming a pre-trained StyleGAN model
from stylegan_utils import generate_image

# Generate an image with a random seed
image = generate_image(seed=42)
image.save("generated_art.png")
```

10.2 Storytelling and Content Creation

AI is transforming storytelling by assisting in creating storyboards, scripts, and enhancing narrative techniques.

10.2.1 AI-Assisted Storyboarding and Scriptwriting

1. Tools for Storyboarding:

- **Storyboard That:** AI-generated storyboards for video production.
- **Plot Generator:** Assists in creating story ideas and plot outlines.

2. AI for Scriptwriting:

- **Applications:** Writing movie scripts, video scripts, and dialogues.
- **Example Workflow:**
    - Input: Scene description.
    - Output: Script draft with dialogues and actions.

Code Example for Scriptwriting Using GPT:

python

```
from langchain.llms import OpenAI
```

```
llm = OpenAI(model="text-davinci-003", api_key="your_api_key")

prompt = """
Write a script for a 30-second ad about a futuristic coffee maker:
Scene 1: A busy morning kitchen.
Scene 2: The coffee maker working autonomously.
"""
response = llm(prompt)
print(response)
```

10.2.2 Enhancing Narrative Techniques with AutoGen

1. Techniques:

- Use AI to refine tone, pacing, and character development.
- Generate alternative endings or plot twists.

2. Benefits:

- Speeds up content creation.
- Encourages experimentation with creative ideas.

10.3 Brainstorming and Idea Generation

AI-powered tools help teams and individuals generate, refine, and evaluate ideas efficiently.

10.3.1 Collaborative AI Tools for Teams

1. Tools for Brainstorming:

- **Miro:** Supports collaborative ideation with AI-driven suggestions.
- **Notion AI:** Assists in note-taking and generating ideas.

2. Features:

- Real-time collaboration.
- Automatic categorization and prioritization of ideas.

10.3.2 Techniques for Maximizing Creativity with AI

1. Techniques:

- Use AI to provide prompts or starting points for brainstorming sessions.
- Implement tools that visualize ideas in mind maps or diagrams.

2. Example: AI-Powered Idea Expansion:

python

```python
prompt = "Generate five innovative ideas for eco-friendly packaging."
response = llm(prompt)
print(response)
```

10.4 Case Studies

10.4.1 Generating Marketing Campaigns for a Startup

Scenario: A startup used AI to generate slogans, ad copy, and visual assets for a product launch.

Outcome:

- Reduced campaign development time by 50%.
- Increased engagement through tailored marketing materials.

10.4.2 Storyboarding for a Media Production Company

Scenario: A media company leveraged AutoGen tools to create storyboards for a TV series.

Outcome:

- Improved efficiency in pre-production planning.
- Enhanced collaboration between writers and designers.

10.5 Hands-On Project

10.5.1 Creating an AI-Powered Brainstorming Tool

Objective: Develop a Python-based tool that uses AI to generate and categorize ideas for a team brainstorming session.

Steps:

1. Collect user input (e.g., topic or problem statement).
2. Use AI to generate ideas.
3. Categorize ideas into themes.

Code Example:

```python
import openai

openai.api_key = "your_api_key"

def brainstorm(topic):
    prompt = f"Generate 10 innovative ideas for {topic}."
    response = openai.Completion.create(
        engine="text-davinci-003",
        prompt=prompt,
        max_tokens=150
    )
```

```
return response['choices'][0]['text']

ideas = brainstorm("sustainable energy solutions")
print("Brainstormed Ideas:\n", ideas)
```

10.6 Practice Problems and Quizzes

10.6.1 Leveraging AI for Creative Processes

Problem: Write a Python script that uses AI to generate and visualize a list of social media post ideas for a product.

10.6.2 Interactive Quizzes

Question: What is the primary role of GANs in art and design?

1. Analyzing customer feedback.
2. Generating realistic images and textures.
3. Creating interactive dashboards.

Answer: 2. Generating realistic images and textures.

10.7 End-of-Chapter Summaries

10.7.1 Key Takeaways

- AI-powered tools like GANs and GPT enhance creative processes in art, design, and storytelling.
- Collaborative AI tools foster innovation in teams.

10.7.2 Quick Reference Guides

- **AI Tools for Art:** DALL-E, Runway ML, StyleGAN.
- **AI Tools for Writing:** OpenAI GPT, Plot Generator.

10.8 Templates and Tools

10.8.1 Workflow Templates

Template for Creative Content Generation:

1. Input: Idea or description.
2. AI Processing: Generate visuals or text.
3. Output: Refined creative assets.

10.8.2 Scripts and Snippets

Reusable Script for Idea Categorization:

python

```python
def categorize_ideas(ideas):
    categories = {}
    for idea in ideas:
        category = input(f"Categorize idea: {idea}")
        categories[idea] = category
    return categories

ideas = ["Reusable packaging", "Solar-powered chargers", "Eco-friendly inks"]
print(categorize_ideas(ideas))
```

This chapter explored how AutoGen systems empower creativity in art, design, storytelling, and brainstorming. With AI-driven tools and techniques, individuals and teams can enhance their creative workflows, generate innovative ideas, and streamline content creation. The provided hands-on project and practical resources offer a starting point for implementing AI in creative ideation.

Chapter 11: Decision Support Systems

Decision Support Systems (DSS) leverage AI and automation to assist in complex decision-making processes, enabling businesses to analyze scenarios, forecast outcomes, and optimize workflows. This chapter provides a comprehensive guide to implementing AI-powered DSS, covering scenario analysis, financial modeling, and business process optimization.

11.1 Automating Scenario Analysis

Scenario analysis evaluates different potential outcomes to support strategic planning. By automating this process, organizations can generate faster and more accurate predictions.

11.1.1 Tools for Predictive Modeling and Simulation

1. Overview of Predictive Modeling:

- **Purpose:** To forecast future trends based on historical data.
- **Common Tools:**
    - **Python Libraries:** Scikit-learn, TensorFlow, PyCaret.
    - **Commercial Software:** SAP Predictive Analytics, RapidMiner.

2. Simulation Techniques:

- Monte Carlo simulations for probabilistic outcomes.
- Scenario planning for best-case, worst-case, and average-case outcomes.

Example Code: Monte Carlo Simulation in Python

python

```python
import numpy as np

# Simulate stock price changes over 10 days
np.random.seed(42)
initial_price = 100
daily_returns = np.random.normal(0.001, 0.02, 10)  # Mean and std deviation
prices = initial_price * (1 + daily_returns).cumprod()

print("Simulated Prices:", prices)
```

3. Benefits of Automating Scenario Analysis:

- Reduces human error.
- Scales to analyze multiple variables simultaneously.

11.1.2 Integrating AI with Business Intelligence (BI) Tools

1. Common BI Tools:

- Tableau, Power BI, Looker.

2. AI Integration Techniques:

- Use APIs to connect predictive models with BI dashboards.
- Automate data fetching and report generation.

Code Example: Integrating AI with Tableau

python

```python
import pandas as pd

# Save predictive model output as CSV for Tableau
data = pd.DataFrame({"Scenario": ["Best", "Worst", "Average"], "Profit": [100000, 50000, 75000]})
```

```
data.to_csv("scenario_analysis.csv", index=False)
print("Data exported for Tableau visualization.")
```

11.2 Financial Modeling and Forecasting

AI enhances financial modeling by automating calculations, generating forecasts, and assessing risks.

11.2.1 Techniques for Automated Financial Analysis

1. Key Techniques:

- Ratio analysis (e.g., profit margins, return on investment).
- Trend analysis for revenue growth.

2. Tools for Financial Analysis:

- Python libraries: Pandas, NumPy, PyPortfolioOpt.

Example Code: Calculating Financial Ratios

python

```
# Example financial data
financials = pd.DataFrame({
    "Revenue": [200000, 250000],
    "Expenses": [150000, 180000]
})

# Calculate profit margin
financials["Profit Margin"] = (financials["Revenue"] - financials["Expenses"]) / financials["Revenue"]
print(financials)
```

11.2.2 Risk Assessment and Management with AI

1. AI Applications in Risk Assessment:

- Identify credit risks using machine learning models.
- Automate fraud detection.

2. Tools:

- **Scikit-learn:** Build classification models for credit risk.
- **TensorFlow:** Create deep learning models for fraud detection.

Example Code: Logistic Regression for Credit Risk

python

```python
from sklearn.linear_model import LogisticRegression
from sklearn.model_selection import train_test_split
from sklearn.metrics import accuracy_score

# Simulated dataset
data = pd.DataFrame({
    "Income": [50000, 60000, 70000, 20000],
    "Debt": [20000, 15000, 10000, 30000],
    "Default": [0, 0, 0, 1]
})

X = data[["Income", "Debt"]]
y = data["Default"]

# Train logistic regression model
X_train, X_test, y_train, y_test = train_test_split(X, y, test_size=0.25)
model = LogisticRegression()
model.fit(X_train, y_train)

# Predict and evaluate
y_pred = model.predict(X_test)
print("Accuracy:", accuracy_score(y_test, y_pred))
```

11.3 Optimizing Business Processes

Automation and AI improve business processes by identifying inefficiencies and suggesting optimal workflows.

11.3.1 Workflow Optimization Algorithms

1. Key Algorithms:

- **Linear Programming:** Solve resource allocation problems.
- **Genetic Algorithms:** Find optimal solutions for complex problems.

Example Code: Linear Programming with PuLP

python

```
from pulp import LpMaximize, LpProblem, LpVariable

# Define problem
problem = LpProblem("Maximize_Profit", LpMaximize)

# Variables
x = LpVariable("Product_A", lowBound=0, cat="Integer")
y = LpVariable("Product_B", lowBound=0, cat="Integer")

# Objective function
problem += 20 * x + 30 * y  # Profit per product

# Constraints
problem += x + 2 * y <= 100  # Resource constraint
problem.solve()

# Print results
```

```python
print(f"Optimal production: Product A={x.value()}, Product B={y.value()}")
```

11.3.2 Implementing AI for Supply Chain Management

1. Applications:

- Demand forecasting using AI models.
- Inventory optimization with predictive analytics.

2. Example Workflow:

- **Input:** Historical sales data.
- **Process:** Predict future demand using machine learning.
- **Output:** Optimize stock levels.

Example Code: Demand Forecasting with ARIMA

python

```python
from statsmodels.tsa.arima.model import ARIMA
import pandas as pd

# Simulated sales data
sales = [120, 130, 125, 140, 150]
model = ARIMA(sales, order=(1, 1, 1))
fit = model.fit()
forecast = fit.forecast(steps=3)
print("Forecasted Demand:", forecast)
```

11.4 Case Studies

11.4.1 Developing a Decision Support Pipeline for Retail

Scenario: A retail chain implemented a decision support pipeline to optimize store inventory and pricing.

Workflow:

1. **Data Collection:** Sales, weather, and regional data.
2. **Analysis:** Predict demand for each store.
3. **Action:** Adjust pricing dynamically.

Outcome:

- Increased revenue by 15%.
- Reduced inventory holding costs by 20%.

11.4.2 Financial Forecasting for an Investment Firm

Scenario: An investment firm used AI to forecast stock performance and identify profitable portfolios.

Workflow:

1. **Input:** Historical stock data.
2. **Analysis:** Risk and return modeling.
3. **Output:** Portfolio recommendations.

Outcome:

- Improved portfolio performance by 25%.
- Reduced risk exposure.

Decision Support Systems powered by AutoGen enable businesses to make informed decisions efficiently. By automating scenario analysis, financial modeling, and business process optimization, these systems deliver tangible improvements in performance and cost-effectiveness. With tools, examples, and case studies, this chapter provides actionable insights for implementing AI-powered DSS in real-world applications.

11.5 Hands-On Project

11.5.1 Building an AI-Driven Decision Support System for a Business

In this project, you will build an **AI-powered Decision Support System (DSS)** for a retail business. The system will help the business make informed decisions about inventory management, demand forecasting, and pricing strategies.

Project Objective: Create a DSS that:

1. Collects and preprocesses sales data.
2. Forecasts product demand using machine learning.
3. Optimizes inventory levels and pricing strategies.
4. Visualizes recommendations in an interactive dashboard.

Step-by-Step Instructions:

Step 1: Set Up the Environment

1. **Install Required Libraries:**

bash

```bash
pip install pandas numpy scikit-learn matplotlib seaborn dash openai
```

2. **Load the Sales Dataset:** Assume a CSV file (sales_data.csv) with the following columns:
    - Date: Date of the transaction.
    - Product: Product name.
    - Sales: Units sold.

- Price: Selling price per unit.

Step 2: Data Preprocessing

Clean and preprocess the data for analysis.

Code Example:

python

```python
import pandas as pd

# Load data
data = pd.read_csv("sales_data.csv")

# Parse dates and fill missing values
data['Date'] = pd.to_datetime(data['Date'])
data['Sales'].fillna(0, inplace=True)
data['Price'].fillna(data['Price'].mean(), inplace=True)

# Preview data
print(data.head())
```

Step 3: Forecasting Demand

Use machine learning to predict future sales.

Code Example:

python

```python
from sklearn.model_selection import train_test_split
from sklearn.ensemble import RandomForestRegressor

# Feature engineering
```

```python
data['Month'] = data['Date'].dt.month
X = data[['Month', 'Price']]
y = data['Sales']

# Train-test split
X_train, X_test, y_train, y_test = train_test_split(X, y, test_size=0.2, random_state=42)

# Train a random forest regressor
model = RandomForestRegressor()
model.fit(X_train, y_train)

# Predict future sales
predictions = model.predict(X_test)
print("Predicted Sales:\n", predictions)
```

Step 4: Optimizing Inventory Levels

Implement inventory optimization based on forecasted demand.

Code Example:

python

```python
def optimize_inventory(demand_forecast, safety_stock=10):
    return demand_forecast + safety_stock

inventory_levels = [optimize_inventory(d) for d in predictions]
print("Optimized Inventory Levels:", inventory_levels)
```

Step 5: Pricing Strategy Optimization

Optimize pricing using linear programming.

Code Example:

```python
from pulp import LpMaximize, LpProblem, LpVariable

# Define the problem
problem = LpProblem("Pricing_Optimization", LpMaximize)

# Variables: Price per product
price = LpVariable("Price", lowBound=5, upBound=50)

# Objective function: Maximize revenue (price * demand)
demand = sum(predictions)  # Total forecasted demand
problem += price * demand

# Solve the problem
problem.solve()

print(f"Optimal Price: ${price.value():.2f}")
```

Step 6: Visualizing Recommendations

Create a dashboard using Dash.

Code Example:

```python
import dash
from dash import html, dcc
import plotly.express as px

# Create a Dash app
app = dash.Dash(__name__)
```

```python
# Create figures
fig_sales = px.line(data, x='Date', y='Sales', title='Historical Sales')
fig_inventory = px.bar(x=range(len(inventory_levels)), y=inventory_levels, title='Optimized Inventory Levels')

# Layout
app.layout = html.Div([
    html.H1("AI-Driven Decision Support System"),
    dcc.Graph(figure=fig_sales),
    dcc.Graph(figure=fig_inventory),
    html.H3(f"Recommended Price: ${price.value():.2f}")
])

if __name__ == "__main__":
    app.run_server(debug=True)
```

Expected Output:

- A dashboard displaying:
    - Historical sales trends.
    - Optimized inventory levels.
    - Recommended pricing strategy.

11.6 Practice Problems and Quizzes

11.6.1 Enhancing Decision-Making with AI Automation

Problem 1: Inventory Management

- Write a function that calculates reorder points for products based on average demand and lead time.

Solution:

python

```
def calculate_reorder_point(average_demand, lead_time, safety_stock=10):
    return (average_demand * lead_time) + safety_stock

# Example usage
reorder_point = calculate_reorder_point(50, 2)
print("Reorder Point:", reorder_point)
```

Problem 2: Demand Forecasting

- Train a machine learning model to forecast sales for multiple products and visualize the predictions.

11.6.2 Interactive Quizzes

Question 1: What is the primary goal of a Decision Support System?

1. Automate customer service.
2. Enhance decision-making with data-driven insights.
3. Predict stock market trends.

Answer: 2. Enhance decision-making with data-driven insights.

Question 2: Which algorithm is best suited for optimizing pricing strategies?

1. Logistic Regression
2. Linear Programming
3. K-Means Clustering

Answer: 2. Linear Programming.

11.7 End-of-Chapter Summaries

11.7.1 Key Takeaways

- AI-powered Decision Support Systems enable efficient and accurate decision-making.
- Techniques like demand forecasting, inventory optimization, and pricing strategies can be automated using AI.
- Dashboards enhance the interpretability of recommendations and insights.

11.7.2 Quick Reference Guides

Task	Tool/Library	Key Functionality
Data Preprocessing	Pandas	Cleaning and organizing data.
Forecasting	Scikit-learn	Predicting future trends.
Optimization	PuLP	Solving pricing and inventory problems.
Visualization	Dash, Plotly	Creating interactive dashboards.

11.8 Templates and Tools

11.8.1 Workflow Templates

Template for DSS Implementation:

1. Collect and preprocess data.
2. Train predictive models.
3. Optimize strategies using mathematical models.
4. Visualize results in a dashboard.

11.8.2 Scripts and Snippets

Reusable Script for Forecasting and Visualization:

python

```python
def forecast_and_visualize(data, model):
    # Train model
    X = data[['Price']]
    y = data['Sales']
    model.fit(X, y)

    # Predict and visualize
    predictions = model.predict(X)
    fig = px.scatter(data, x='Price', y='Sales', title='Sales vs Price')
    fig.add_scatter(x=data['Price'], y=predictions, mode='lines', name='Forecast')
    fig.show()
```

This chapter demonstrated how to build an AI-driven Decision Support System (DSS) for businesses. By automating scenario analysis, financial modeling, and process optimization, AI enables organizations to make smarter, faster decisions. The hands-on project, practice problems, and reusable templates provide a solid foundation for applying AI in real-world decision-making contexts.

Chapter 12: Knowledge Management

Knowledge management involves organizing, summarizing, and leveraging information effectively to enhance productivity, decision-making, and collaboration. AutoGen systems are at the forefront of this transformation, enabling the creation of knowledge graphs, summaries, and accessible repositories. This chapter delves into the techniques, tools, and real-world applications of AI-driven knowledge management.

12.1 Organizing and Summarizing Information

Efficient knowledge organization and summarization are essential for extracting actionable insights from vast datasets.

12.1.1 AI Techniques for Knowledge Extraction

1. **Techniques:**

   - **Natural Language Processing (NLP):** Extracts key points from text using entity recognition, summarization, and sentiment analysis.

   - **Topic Modeling:** Groups related topics within large datasets.

2. **Tools:**

   - **SpaCy:** For entity extraction and processing.

   - **Hugging Face Transformers:** For generating summaries using pre-trained models.

Code Example: Extracting Entities with SpaCy

python

```python
import spacy

# Load SpaCy model
nlp = spacy.load("en_core_web_sm")

# Sample text
text = "Elon Musk announced a new Tesla factory in Berlin."

# Process text
doc = nlp(text)

# Extract entities
for ent in doc.ents:
    print(f"{ent.text} ({ent.label_})")
```

Expected Output:

scss

Elon Musk (PERSON)

Tesla (ORG)

Berlin (GPE)

3. Applications:

- Automating information extraction from documents, emails, and research papers.
- Summarizing customer feedback or meeting notes.

12.1.2 Creating Accessible Knowledge Repositories

1. Characteristics of a Good Knowledge Repository:

- **Searchable:** Easily find relevant information.
- **Organized:** Structured categories and tags.
- **Interactive:** Allow updates and user contributions.

2. Tools for Building Repositories:
- **ElasticSearch:** For creating powerful search engines.
- **Notion/Confluence:** Collaborative knowledge-sharing platforms.

Code Example: Indexing Knowledge with ElasticSearch

python

```python
from elasticsearch import Elasticsearch

# Initialize ElasticSearch client
es = Elasticsearch()

# Index a document
doc = {
    "title": "AI in Healthcare",
    "content": "AI is revolutionizing diagnostics and patient care."
}
es.index(index="knowledge_repo", id=1, document=doc)

# Search the repository
res = es.search(index="knowledge_repo", query={"match": {"content": "AI"}})
print(res['hits']['hits'])
```

12.2 Building Knowledge Graphs

Knowledge graphs represent entities and their relationships, providing a visual and structural way to organize complex information.

12.2.1 Fundamentals of Knowledge Graphs

1. Key Components:

- **Nodes:** Represent entities (e.g., people, places, concepts).
- **Edges:** Represent relationships (e.g., "works at," "located in").

2. Benefits:

- Simplifies complex data relationships.
- Enhances searchability and context understanding.

3. Use Cases:

- Search engines like Google.
- Organizational knowledge management.

12.2.2 Tools and Frameworks for Graph Construction

1. Tools:

- **Neo4j:** A graph database for storing and querying large-scale graphs.
- **NetworkX:** A Python library for graph manipulation.

2. Code Example: Building a Knowledge Graph

python

```python
import networkx as nx

# Create a directed graph
graph = nx.DiGraph()

# Add nodes and edges
```

```
graph.add_edge("Tesla", "Berlin", relation="Factory Location")
graph.add_edge("Elon Musk", "Tesla", relation="CEO")

# Display relationships
for edge in graph.edges(data=True):
    print(f"{edge[0]} -[{edge[2]['relation']}]-> {edge[1]}")
```

Expected Output:

css

Tesla -[Factory Location]-> Berlin
Elon Musk -[CEO]-> Tesla

12.3 Automating Technical and Academic Research Summaries

12.3.1 Natural Language Processing (NLP) for Research

1. Applications:

- Extracting abstracts and key findings from academic papers.
- Summarizing technical documentation for quick comprehension.

2. Tools:

- **Semantic Scholar API:** Access research papers and extract metadata.
- **BERT-Based Models:** Generate accurate and concise summaries.

Example: Summarizing Research with Hugging Face Transformers

python

```
from transformers import pipeline
```

```python
# Load summarization pipeline
summarizer = pipeline("summarization")

# Sample text
text = """
Artificial intelligence is transforming healthcare through the use of predictive analytics,
personalized medicine, and automated diagnostics.
"""

# Generate summary
summary = summarizer(text, max_length=50, min_length=25, do_sample=False)
print("Summary:", summary[0]['summary_text'])
```

12.3.2 Enhancing Research Productivity with AI

1. Strategies:

- Use AI to identify gaps in existing research.
- Automate literature reviews and citation management.

2. Example: Citation Recommendation with GPT

python

```
from langchain.llms import OpenAI

# Initialize OpenAI
llm = OpenAI(model="text-davinci-003", api_key="your_api_key")

# Generate citation suggestions
prompt = "Suggest recent citations for a paper on AI ethics."
```

```
response = llm(prompt)
print("Suggested Citations:\n", response)
```

12.4 Case Studies

12.4.1 Automating Technical FAQ Generation for a Tech Support Team

Scenario: A tech company automated its FAQ creation by extracting common customer queries and pairing them with answers from a knowledge base.

Outcome:

- Reduced support response time by 40%.
- Increased self-service query resolution by 60%.

12.4.2 Creating a Knowledge Graph for an Academic Institution

Scenario: An academic institution used knowledge graphs to link researchers, publications, and projects.

Outcome:

- Simplified collaboration across departments.
- Improved access to research expertise.

12.5 Hands-On Project

12.5.1 Developing an AI-Powered Technical FAQ Generator

Objective: Create a system that generates FAQs from a dataset of customer queries and responses.

Steps:
1. Preprocess customer queries.
2. Cluster similar queries using machine learning.
3. Pair queries with responses to generate FAQs.

Code Example:

python

```python
from sklearn.feature_extraction.text import TfidfVectorizer
from sklearn.cluster import KMeans

# Sample data
queries = [
    "How to reset my password?",
    "How do I recover a lost password?",
    "What are the payment options?",
    "Can I pay via PayPal?"
]

# Vectorize queries
vectorizer = TfidfVectorizer()
X = vectorizer.fit_transform(queries)

# Cluster queries
kmeans = KMeans(n_clusters=2)
kmeans.fit(X)

# Print clusters
for i, label in enumerate(kmeans.labels_):
    print(f"Query: {queries[i]} - Cluster: {label}")
```

12.6 Practice Problems and Quizzes

12.6.1 Mastering Knowledge Management with AutoGen

Problem: Write a script to identify key entities and relationships from a dataset of news articles.

12.6.2 Interactive Quizzes

Question: What is the primary advantage of a knowledge graph?

1. Stores data in a flat structure.
2. Represents entities and their relationships.
3. Automates hardware configurations.

Answer: 2. Represents entities and their relationships.

12.7 End-of-Chapter Summaries

12.7.1 Key Takeaways

- Knowledge management systems improve information organization and accessibility.
- AI-powered tools like NLP and knowledge graphs simplify information extraction and visualization.

12.7.2 Quick Reference Guides

Task	Tool/Library	Key Functionality
Entity Extraction	SpaCy	Extracts entities from text.
Knowledge Graphs	NetworkX, Neo4j	Constructs and queries graphs.
Summarization	Hugging Face	Generates concise text

Task	Tool/Library	Key Functionality
	Transformers	summaries.

12.8 Templates and Tools

12.8.1 Workflow Templates

Template for Automating Knowledge Extraction:

1. Input: Raw documents or datasets.
2. Process: Extract entities and summarize content.
3. Output: Organized repository or knowledge graph.

12.8.2 Scripts and Snippets

Reusable Script for Summarizing Large Text Files:

python

```python
def summarize_file(file_path):
    with open(file_path, 'r') as file:
        text = file.read()
    summary = summarizer(text, max_length=100, min_length=50, do_sample=False)
    return summary[0]['summary_text']

# Example usage
print(summarize_file("document.txt"))
```

This chapter explored AI-driven knowledge management, covering information extraction, knowledge graph creation, and research automation. With practical tools, examples, and a hands-on project, you are now equipped to build scalable knowledge management systems for various domains.

Chapter 13: Personalized Education and Training

Personalized education and training are revolutionizing how individuals learn and grow, both academically and professionally. With the help of AI, content can now be tailored to individual needs, learning paths can be optimized, and progress can be tracked automatically. This chapter explores AI-driven adaptive learning systems, corporate training automation, and the integration of AI in academic settings.

13.1 Tailoring Learning Content for Individual Needs

13.1.1 Adaptive Learning Systems

1. What Are Adaptive Learning Systems?

- Adaptive learning systems dynamically adjust the content and pace of lessons based on the learner's performance, preferences, and needs.
- These systems utilize machine learning algorithms to analyze data and recommend the next steps.

2. Features of Adaptive Learning:

- **Real-Time Adjustments:** Modify difficulty levels based on learner responses.
- **Personalized Content:** Focus on topics where learners struggle.
- **Engagement Tracking:** Monitor progress and adapt the format to retain interest.

3. Tools and Platforms:

- **Smart Sparrow:** An adaptive learning platform.

- **Knewton:** Provides AI-driven learning content recommendations.

Code Example: Adaptive Quiz Generator

python

```
import random

# Question bank
questions = {
    "easy": ["What is 2+2?", "Name a primary color."],
    "medium": ["What is the capital of France?", "What is 15*2?"],
    "hard": ["Explain Newton's second law of motion.", "What is the derivative of x^2?"]
}

# Adaptive quiz function
def generate_quiz(level):
    return random.choice(questions[level])

# Example usage
performance_level = "medium"  # Adjust based on learner's performance
print("Question:", generate_quiz(performance_level))
```

13.1.2 Personalized Study Plans with AI

1. Role of AI in Study Plans:

- Analyzes student data such as strengths, weaknesses, and learning preferences.
- Creates schedules and plans focusing on improvement areas.

2. Example Workflow:

1. Input: Test scores, topics of interest.
2. AI Process: Analyze performance and prioritize topics.
3. Output: A daily or weekly study plan.

Code Example: Personalized Study Plan Generator

python

```
def create_study_plan(topics, performance):
    # Sort topics based on performance
    sorted_topics = sorted(topics, key=lambda x: performance[x])
    plan = {day: topic for day, topic in enumerate(sorted_topics, 1)}
    return plan

# Example data
topics = ["Math", "Science", "History"]
performance = {"Math": 70, "Science": 50, "History": 90}  # Lower scores need more focus

study_plan = create_study_plan(topics, performance)
print("Personalized Study Plan:", study_plan)
```

13.2 Corporate Training and Development

13.2.1 Automating Training Modules

1. Automating Content Delivery:

- AI systems deliver training materials, quizzes, and interactive exercises.
- Content is adapted based on the learner's job role and proficiency level.

2. Tools:

- **Articulate 360:** Automates the creation of e-learning content.
- **Coursera for Business:** Offers AI-driven corporate training.

Code Example: Automating Training Module Selection

python

```python
def recommend_training(role):
    training_modules = {
        "developer": ["Advanced Python", "Machine Learning Basics"],
        "manager": ["Leadership Skills", "Project Management"],
    }
    return training_modules.get(role, "General Orientation")

# Example usage
employee_role = "developer"
print("Recommended Training Modules:", recommend_training(employee_role))
```

13.2.2 Measuring Training Effectiveness with AI

1. Metrics for Effectiveness:
- Completion rates.
- Quiz and test scores.
- Post-training performance improvements.

2. AI for Analysis:
- Sentiment analysis on feedback forms.
- Correlating training completion with key performance indicators (KPIs).

Code Example: Tracking Training Effectiveness

```python
import numpy as np

# Training scores before and after
before_training = [70, 80, 60, 90]
after_training = [85, 90, 75, 95]

# Calculate improvement
improvement = np.mean(after_training) - np.mean(before_training)
print("Average Improvement:", improvement)
```

13.3 Enhancing Academic Settings

13.3.1 AI Tutors and Assistants

1. Capabilities of AI Tutors:
- Answer student questions in real time.
- Provide explanations and examples.
- Assist with homework and test preparation.

2. Tools:
- **Socratic by Google:** An AI tutor for school-level subjects.
- **Khan Academy's AI Assistant:** Personalized guidance on learning topics.

Code Example: Simple AI Tutor

```python
from transformers import pipeline

# Load Q&A pipeline
```

```python
qa_pipeline = pipeline("question-answering")

# Example Q&A
context = "The mitochondria is the powerhouse of the cell."
question = "What is the mitochondria?"
answer = qa_pipeline(question=question, context=context)
print("Answer:", answer['answer'])
```

13.3.2 Automating Grading and Feedback

1. Benefits:

- Saves time for educators.
- Provides detailed, consistent feedback.

2. Tools:

- **Gradescope:** Automates grading for exams and assignments.
- **Turnitin:** Assesses originality and provides feedback.

Code Example: Automated Grading Script

python

```python
def grade_answers(answers, correct_answers):
    grades = [1 if ans == correct_ans else 0 for ans, correct_ans in zip(answers, correct_answers)]
    return sum(grades) / len(grades) * 100

# Example usage
student_answers = ["A", "B", "C", "D"]
correct_answers = ["A", "C", "C", "D"]
print("Grade:", grade_answers(student_answers, correct_answers), "%")
```

13.4 Case Studies

13.4.1 Creating Personalized Study Guides for Students

Scenario: A university deployed an AI system to create customized study guides based on students' grades and learning preferences.

Outcome:

- Improved exam performance by 25%.
- Increased engagement with tailored content.

13.4.2 Implementing AI-Driven Corporate Training Programs

Scenario: A multinational corporation used AI to automate training modules for onboarding and skill development.

Outcome:

- Reduced training costs by 40%.
- Faster employee onboarding.

13.5 Hands-On Project

13.5.1 Building a Personalized Study Guide Generator

Objective: Develop a tool that generates personalized study guides based on topics and learner performance.

Steps:

1. Input student data (e.g., test scores, topics).
2. Rank topics by priority.
3. Output a structured study guide.

Code Example:

python

```python
def generate_study_guide(topics, scores):
    guide = {topic: "High Priority" if score < 50 else "Low Priority" for topic, score in zip(topics, scores)}
    return guide

# Example usage
topics = ["Math", "Science", "History"]
scores = [40, 60, 30]  # Scores out of 100
study_guide = generate_study_guide(topics, scores)
print("Study Guide:", study_guide)
```

13.6 Practice Problems and Quizzes

13.6.1 Designing AI-Powered Educational Tools

Problem: Design a system that recommends study materials based on quiz performance.

13.6.2 Interactive Quizzes

Question: What is a key feature of adaptive learning systems?

1. Fixed content delivery.
2. Adjusts based on learner's performance.
3. Requires manual intervention.

Answer: 2. Adjusts based on learner's performance.

13.7 End-of-Chapter Summaries

13.7.1 Key Takeaways

- AI enables personalized education by tailoring content and tracking progress.
- Adaptive learning systems and AI tutors enhance learning experiences.

13.7.2 Quick Reference Guides

Task	Tool/Library	Key Functionality
Adaptive Learning	Python, Knewton	Generates dynamic learning paths.
Automated Grading	Gradescope, Custom Code	Grades assignments and quizzes.

13.8 Templates and Tools

13.8.1 Workflow Templates

Template for Personalized Education:

1. Input: Learner's performance data.
2. Process: Analyze data and generate study plan.
3. Output: Custom study guides or training modules.

13.8.2 Scripts and Snippets

Reusable Script for Quiz Analysis:

python

```
def analyze_quiz_performance(scores, threshold=50):
    feedback = ["Needs Improvement" if score < threshold else "Good Job" for score in scores]
```

    return feedback

# Example usage
scores = [40, 75, 60, 30]
print("Feedback:", analyze_quiz_performance(scores))

This chapter explored how AI transforms education and training through personalized content, adaptive learning systems, and automated tools. With hands-on projects and practical examples, readers can now implement AI-driven solutions in various educational contexts.

Chapter 14: Prototyping and Simulation

Prototyping and simulation are essential steps in the development of AI-driven systems. They enable developers and teams to test ideas, validate workflows, and identify potential issues before full-scale implementation. AutoGen systems play a critical role in accelerating these processes by automating repetitive tasks and providing tools for rapid prototyping and simulation. This chapter explores the techniques, tools, and practical applications of prototyping and simulation with AutoGen.

14.1 Accelerating Concept Testing with AutoGen

14.1.1 Rapid Prototyping Techniques

1. What is Rapid Prototyping?

- Rapid prototyping involves quickly creating a functional model of a system or workflow to test its feasibility and gather feedback.
- In the context of AI, it includes building minimal viable models (MVMs) for algorithms and workflows.

2. Key Techniques:

- **Low-Fidelity Prototypes:** Using simple tools like flowcharts or mockups.
- **High-Fidelity Prototypes:** Developing functional models with real datasets and tools.
- **Iterative Refinement:** Continuously improving the prototype based on feedback.

3. Tools for Rapid Prototyping:

- **Jupyter Notebooks:** For creating and testing machine learning models quickly.
- **Streamlit/Gradio:** For building interactive AI demos.

Code Example: Simple Prototype Using Streamlit

python

```python
import streamlit as st

# Prototype for a sentiment analysis tool
st.title("Sentiment Analysis Prototype")
text = st.text_input("Enter text for analysis:")

if text:
    # Dummy analysis
    sentiment = "Positive" if "good" in text else "Negative"
    st.write(f"Sentiment: {sentiment}")
```

14.1.2 Simulating AI-Driven Workflows

1. Workflow Simulation:

- Simulations allow you to test the behavior of AI systems in a controlled environment.
- They are particularly useful for multi-agent systems, supply chains, and predictive models.

2. Steps for Workflow Simulation:

1. Define the process to simulate (e.g., a customer support system).
2. Create a virtual environment to mimic real-world conditions.
3. Test different scenarios to evaluate performance.

Code Example: Simulating a Simple Customer Support Workflow

```python
import random

# Simulate customer queries
queries = ["Billing issue", "Technical support", "Account cancellation"]

def handle_query(query):
    if query == "Billing issue":
        return "Redirected to Billing Team"
    elif query == "Technical support":
        return "Redirected to Technical Support Team"
    else:
        return "Redirected to Retention Team"

# Run simulation
for query in queries:
    print(f"Query: {query} -> Response: {handle_query(query)}")
```

14.2 Examples of Rapid AI Prototyping

14.2.1 From Idea to Prototype: Case Studies

Case Study 1: Developing a Chatbot for Healthcare

- **Objective:** Build a prototype chatbot for scheduling medical appointments.

- **Process:**
    - Define key functions (e.g., appointment booking, reminders).
    - Use GPT for natural language understanding.
- **Outcome:** A working prototype was delivered in one week, enabling stakeholder feedback.

Case Study 2: AI-Powered Inventory Management

- **Objective:** Optimize stock levels using predictive analytics.
- **Process:**
    - Create a minimal dataset and test prediction algorithms.
    - Simulate inventory changes based on demand.
- **Outcome:** Identified inefficiencies and optimized the final model.

14.2.2 Best Practices for Efficient Prototyping

1. Start Small: Focus on one key feature. **2. Use Existing Tools:** Avoid reinventing the wheel by leveraging libraries and frameworks. **3. Gather Feedback Early:** Share prototypes with stakeholders to refine requirements.

14.3 Tools for Simulation and Testing

14.3.1 Virtual Environments and Simulators

1. What Are Virtual Environments?

- Controlled digital spaces where AI models and workflows can be tested safely.

2. Common Simulators:

- **Unity ML-Agents:** For simulating environments in gaming or robotics.
- **OpenAI Gym:** For testing reinforcement learning algorithms.

Code Example: Using OpenAI Gym

python

```python
import gym

# Create a simulation environment
env = gym.make("CartPole-v1")
state = env.reset()

# Simulate an agent's actions
for _ in range(10):
    action = env.action_space.sample()  # Random action
    state, reward, done, _ = env.step(action)
    if done:
        state = env.reset()
env.close()
```

14.3.2 Integrating AutoGen with Simulation Tools

1. Example Use Case: Multi-Agent Systems

- Use AutoGen to define agent behaviors and simulate their interactions.

2. Code Example: Agent Behavior Simulation

python

```python
class Agent:
    def __init__(self, name):
```

```
    self.name = name

  def act(self, environment):
    return f"{self.name} interacts with {environment}"

# Simulate agent interactions
agents = [Agent("Agent A"), Agent("Agent B")]
environment = "virtual workspace"
for agent in agents:
  print(agent.act(environment))
```

14.4 Case Studies

14.4.1 Simulating Agent Workflows for a Virtual Assistant

Scenario: A tech company simulated a virtual assistant's interactions with users to test its natural language understanding.

Outcome:

- Identified gaps in intent recognition.
- Improved the assistant's conversational capabilities.

14.4.2 Prototyping AI Solutions for a Manufacturing Process

Scenario: An automotive manufacturer used AI simulations to optimize production line efficiency.

Outcome:

- Reduced downtime by 20%.
- Improved overall productivity.

14.5 Hands-On Project

14.5.1 Developing a Simulated Agent Workflow in a Virtual Environment

Objective: Build a simulation of a multi-agent system for managing tasks in a virtual workspace.

Steps:

1. Define the agents and their roles.
2. Create a virtual environment.
3. Simulate interactions and analyze results.

Code Example:

python

```python
class Task:
    def __init__(self, name):
        self.name = name
        self.assigned_to = None

    def assign(self, agent):
        self.assigned_to = agent
        return f"Task '{self.name}' assigned to {agent}"

tasks = [Task("Data Analysis"), Task("Report Writing")]
agents = ["Agent A", "Agent B"]

# Assign tasks
for task, agent in zip(tasks, agents):
    print(task.assign(agent))
```

14.6 Practice Problems and Quizzes

14.6.1 Enhancing Prototyping Skills with AutoGen

Problem: Simulate the workflow of a logistics system where tasks are assigned to delivery agents based on their proximity to the pickup location.

14.6.2 Interactive Quizzes

Question: What is the primary benefit of using virtual environments for simulation?

1. Reduces computational cost.
2. Provides controlled testing conditions.
3. Eliminates the need for real-world implementation.

Answer: 2. Provides controlled testing conditions.

14.7 End-of-Chapter Summaries

14.7.1 Key Takeaways

- Rapid prototyping and simulation save time and resources during AI development.
- Tools like OpenAI Gym and Unity ML-Agents enable comprehensive testing in virtual environments.

14.7.2 Quick Reference Guides

Task	Tool/Library	Key Functionality
Workflow Simulation	OpenAI Gym	Test reinforcement learning models.
Agent Behavior	Python Custom	Model and simulate agent

Task	Tool/Library	Key Functionality
Simulation	Scripts	actions.

14.8 Templates and Tools

14.8.1 Workflow Templates

Template for Simulation:

1. Define the environment.
2. Create agents and workflows.
3. Simulate and collect performance metrics.

14.8.2 Scripts and Snippets

Reusable Script for Task Assignment:

python

```python
def assign_tasks(agents, tasks):
    assignments = {agent: task for agent, task in zip(agents, tasks)}
    return assignments

# Example usage
agents = ["Agent A", "Agent B"]
tasks = ["Task 1", "Task 2"]
print("Assignments:", assign_tasks(agents, tasks))
```

Prototyping and simulation are invaluable for testing AI-driven workflows and systems. By leveraging tools, frameworks, and methodologies outlined in this chapter, you can create robust prototypes and simulate their performance in controlled environments. With practice problems and hands-on projects, this chapter equips you with the skills to accelerate concept testing and development.

Part III: Advanced Topics and Emerging Trends

Chapter 15: Integrating AutoGen with Emerging Technologies

Emerging technologies such as the Internet of Things (IoT), blockchain, and edge computing are transforming industries by enabling smarter, more connected systems. AutoGen provides powerful capabilities to automate, enhance, and streamline workflows in these technologies. This chapter explores how AutoGen integrates with IoT, blockchain, and edge computing, complete with real-world applications, tools, and hands-on projects.

15.1 Internet of Things (IoT) and AutoGen

15.1.1 Automating IoT Device Management

1. IoT Device Management Challenges:

- Managing thousands of interconnected devices.
- Ensuring secure communication and firmware updates.
- Monitoring performance and resolving issues in real time.

2. Role of AutoGen:

- Automates provisioning, configuration, and monitoring of IoT devices.
- Facilitates remote diagnostics and updates using AI-driven workflows.

Code Example: Automating IoT Device Provisioning

python

```python
import paho.mqtt.client as mqtt
```

```python
# MQTT callback for connection
def on_connect(client, userdata, flags, rc):
    print("Connected with result code", rc)
    client.subscribe("iot/device/register")

# Automate provisioning
def on_message(client, userdata, msg):
    device_id = msg.payload.decode()
    print(f"Provisioning device: {device_id}")
    # Simulate provisioning logic
    client.publish(f"iot/device/{device_id}/status", "Provisioned")

# MQTT client setup
client = mqtt.Client()
client.on_connect = on_connect
client.on_message = on_message
client.connect("broker.hivemq.com", 1883, 60)
client.loop_forever()
```

3. Benefits:

- Reduces manual intervention in managing IoT devices.
- Ensures consistent configurations across the network.

15.1.2 Data Collection and Analysis from IoT Networks

1. Automated Data Pipelines:

- AutoGen automates data ingestion from IoT devices into cloud storage or analytics platforms.
- AI models analyze data to predict failures, optimize performance, and provide insights.

Code Example: Collecting IoT Data and Analyzing Trends

python

```python
import pandas as pd

# Sample IoT data
data = {
    "timestamp": ["2024-01-01 12:00", "2024-01-01 12:10", "2024-01-01 12:20"],
    "temperature": [22.5, 23.0, 22.8]
}
df = pd.DataFrame(data)

# Analyze trends
average_temp = df["temperature"].mean()
print("Average Temperature:", average_temp)
```

15.2 Blockchain and Smart Contracts

15.2.1 Enhancing Security and Transparency with AutoGen

1. Blockchain Benefits:

- Immutable records ensure trust.
- Decentralized architecture enhances resilience.

2. AutoGen Applications:

- Automates the creation and deployment of secure blockchain solutions.
- Verifies transactions using AI-driven logic.

Code Example: Automating Blockchain Record Verification

python

```
from web3 import Web3
```

```python
# Connect to blockchain
web3 = Web3(Web3.HTTPProvider("http://127.0.0.1:8545"))

# Verify a transaction
def verify_transaction(tx_hash):
    tx = web3.eth.get_transaction(tx_hash)
    print(f"Transaction Details: {tx}")

# Example usage
verify_transaction("0x123...abc")
```

15.2.2 Automating Smart Contract Deployment and Management

1. Smart Contracts:

- Self-executing agreements with predefined rules.
- AutoGen streamlines deployment and monitoring.

Code Example: Deploying a Smart Contract

solidity

```solidity
// Simple Smart Contract
pragma solidity ^0.8.0;

contract HelloWorld {
    string public message = "Hello, Blockchain!";
}
```

Python Script to Deploy Contract:

python

```python
from web3 import Web3
```

```python
from solcx import compile_source

# Compile contract
contract_source = '''
pragma solidity ^0.8.0;
contract HelloWorld {
    string public message = "Hello, Blockchain!";
}
'''
compiled = compile_source(contract_source)
contract_interface = compiled['<stdin>:HelloWorld']

# Connect to blockchain
web3 = Web3(Web3.HTTPProvider("http://127.0.0.1:8545"))
web3.eth.default_account = web3.eth.accounts[0]

# Deploy contract
HelloWorld = web3.eth.contract(abi=contract_interface['abi'], bytecode=contract_interface['bin'])
tx_hash = HelloWorld.constructor().transact()
tx_receipt = web3.eth.wait_for_transaction_receipt(tx_hash)
print("Contract Deployed at:", tx_receipt.contractAddress)
```

15.3 Edge Computing and AutoGen

15.3.1 Distributed Workflow Automation

1. Edge Computing Overview:

- Processes data closer to devices, reducing latency and bandwidth usage.
- Ideal for IoT and real-time applications.

2. AutoGen Role:

- Automates the deployment of workflows across edge devices.
- Balances workloads between cloud and edge nodes.

15.3.2 Real-Time Data Processing and Decision-Making

1. Use Case: Traffic Management

- AutoGen processes real-time traffic data at edge nodes.
- Provides actionable insights like rerouting or signaling changes.

Code Example: Real-Time Data Aggregation

python

```
import numpy as np

# Simulate edge data processing
data_stream = np.random.rand(100)  # Random traffic data
avg_traffic = np.mean(data_stream)
print("Average Traffic Level:", avg_traffic)
```

15.4 Case Studies

15.4.1 Automating IoT Device Coordination in Smart Homes

Scenario: AutoGen automated the management of IoT devices in a smart home ecosystem, coordinating lighting, HVAC, and security systems.

Outcome:

- Reduced energy consumption by 30%.
- Improved user convenience.

15.4.2 Implementing AutoGen for Blockchain-Based Supply Chains

Scenario: A logistics company used AutoGen to automate tracking and verification of goods using blockchain.

Outcome:

- Increased transparency across the supply chain.
- Reduced fraud and disputes.

15.5 Hands-On Project

15.5.1 Building an AI-Driven IoT Device Management System

Objective: Develop a system to automate the management of IoT devices, including registration, monitoring, and updates.

Steps:

1. Set up MQTT for device communication.
2. Use AutoGen to automate monitoring and alerts.

Code Example: Monitoring IoT Devices

python

```
import time

devices = {"Device1": "Online", "Device2": "Offline"}

# Monitor devices
def monitor_devices():
    while True:
        for device, status in devices.items():
```

```
        print(f"{device}: {status}")
    time.sleep(5)

monitor_devices()
```

15.6 Practice Problems and Quizzes

15.6.1 Integrating AutoGen with Emerging Technologies

Problem: Write a script to simulate real-time data from IoT sensors and process it for anomalies.

15.6.2 Interactive Quizzes

Question: What is the primary advantage of edge computing?

1. Centralized data processing.
2. Reduced latency and real-time insights.
3. Increased bandwidth usage.

Answer: 2. Reduced latency and real-time insights.

15.7 Platform-Specific Integrations

15.7.1 Detailed Sub-Sections for AWS, Azure, and Google Cloud

1. AWS IoT Core Integration:

- Automates device management and data processing workflows.

2. Azure IoT Hub Integration:

- Provides real-time monitoring and analytics for IoT networks.

3. Google Cloud IoT Core:

- Integrates AutoGen for edge-to-cloud workflows.

15.7.2 Actionable Insights and Examples for Each Platform

Example Workflow for AWS IoT:

python

```python
import boto3

# Initialize IoT client
iot_client = boto3.client('iot')

# List IoT devices
devices = iot_client.list_things()
print("Devices:", devices)
```

15.8 End-of-Chapter Summaries

15.8.1 Key Takeaways

- AutoGen accelerates the integration of emerging technologies like IoT, blockchain, and edge computing.
- Real-world applications demonstrate its value in improving efficiency and reducing costs.

15.8.2 Quick Reference Guides

Task	Tool/Library	Key Functionality

Task	Tool/Library	Key Functionality
IoT Device Management	Paho MQTT	Automates IoT workflows.
Blockchain Deployment	Web3.py	Deploys and manages smart contracts.
Edge Data Processing	Python, NumPy	Analyzes real-time data streams.

15.9 Templates and Tools

15.9.1 Workflow Templates

Template for IoT Automation:

1. Connect devices to an MQTT broker.
2. Automate monitoring and alerts.
3. Process data and send insights to the cloud.

15.9.2 Scripts and Snippets

Reusable Script for Device Status Monitoring:

python

```python
def check_device_status(devices):
    for device, status in devices.items():
        if status == "Offline":
            print(f"Alert: {device} is offline!")
```

This chapter illustrated how AutoGen integrates with emerging technologies to automate workflows, enhance security, and improve efficiency. By combining IoT, blockchain, and edge computing, AutoGen enables cutting-edge solutions for diverse industries.

Chapter 16: Scaling and Optimizing AutoGen Systems

Scaling and optimizing AutoGen systems are critical for ensuring their performance, reliability, and cost-effectiveness as workloads grow. This chapter explores strategies for scaling infrastructure, tuning performance, managing costs, and designing flexible systems that can adapt to changing demands. It includes case studies, hands-on projects, and practical tools to help implement scalable and optimized AutoGen systems.

16.1 Scaling Infrastructure for AutoGen

16.1.1 Cloud vs. On-Premises Solutions

1. Cloud Solutions:

- **Advantages:**
    - Elastic scaling: Adjust resources based on demand.
    - Managed services: Reduce operational overhead.
    - Global reach: Deploy applications closer to users.
- **Challenges:**
    - Potential latency for edge use cases.
    - Long-term costs for sustained workloads.

2. On-Premises Solutions:

- **Advantages:**
    - Greater control over data security.
    - Lower costs for predictable workloads.
- **Challenges:**

- Requires significant upfront investment.
- Limited scalability compared to cloud solutions.

Comparison Table: Cloud vs. On-Premises

Feature	Cloud	On-Premises
Scalability	Elastic	Limited
Initial Costs	Low	High
Maintenance	Managed by provider	Requires in-house team
Security	Provider-dependent	Fully controlled

16.1.2 Managing Compute Resources Efficiently

1. Techniques for Resource Management:

- **Auto-Scaling:** Automatically adjusts compute resources based on workload.
- **Containerization:** Use Docker and Kubernetes to maximize resource utilization.
- **Spot Instances:** Leverage discounted compute instances for non-critical tasks.

Code Example: Auto-Scaling with AWS Lambda

python

```
import boto3

# Create Lambda client
lambda_client = boto3.client('lambda')

# Update concurrency limit
response = lambda_client.put_function_concurrency(
    FunctionName='my_autogen_function',
```

```
    ReservedConcurrentExecutions=10
)
print("Concurrency updated:", response)
```

16.2 Performance Tuning and Optimization

16.2.1 Techniques for Enhancing AI Model Performance

1. Model Optimization Techniques:

- **Quantization:** Reduce model size by converting weights from floating-point to integer.
- **Pruning:** Remove redundant parameters to improve efficiency.
- **Knowledge Distillation:** Train smaller models using outputs from larger models.

Code Example: Quantization with PyTorch

python

```
import torch
from torchvision import models

# Load model
model = models.resnet18(pretrained=True)

# Quantize model
model.eval()
quantized_model = torch.quantization.quantize_dynamic(
    model, {torch.nn.Linear}, dtype=torch.qint8
)
print("Quantized model size:", quantized_model)
```

16.2.2 Optimizing Workflow Efficiency

1. Techniques:

- Use parallel processing for data-heavy tasks.
- Cache intermediate results to avoid redundant computations.
- Minimize API calls by batching requests.

Code Example: Parallel Processing with Python

python

```
from multiprocessing import Pool

# Function to process data
def process_data(data):
    return data * 2

# Input data
data = [1, 2, 3, 4, 5]

# Parallel processing
with Pool(4) as pool:
    results = pool.map(process_data, data)
print("Processed data:", results)
```

16.3 Cost Management and Optimization

16.3.1 Budgeting for AI-Driven Automation

1. Cost Drivers:

- Compute resources (e.g., VMs, GPUs).
- Data storage and transfer.

- Licensing for AutoGen platforms.

2. Budgeting Tips:
- Use cost estimation tools provided by cloud providers.
- Allocate budgets to high-impact workflows.

16.3.2 Strategies for Reducing Operational Costs

1. Optimize Resource Allocation:
- Rightsize compute instances to match workload demands.
- Use serverless architectures for sporadic tasks.

2. Reduce Redundancy:
- Consolidate workflows where possible.
- Use deduplication for storage efficiency.

Code Example: Monitoring Costs with AWS Cost Explorer

python

```python
import boto3

# Initialize Cost Explorer client
ce_client = boto3.client('ce')

# Get cost and usage
response = ce_client.get_cost_and_usage(
    TimePeriod={'Start': '2024-01-01', 'End': '2024-01-31'},
    Granularity='MONTHLY',
    Metrics=['BlendedCost']
)
print("Monthly Cost:", response['ResultsByTime'][0]['Total']['BlendedCost']['Amount'])
```

16.4 Ensuring Scalability and Flexibility

16.4.1 Designing Modular and Extensible Systems

1. Key Principles:

- **Separation of Concerns:** Design components to handle specific tasks.
- **APIs for Integration:** Use standardized interfaces for communication.

2. Example: Modular Workflow Design

- A data pipeline with separate modules for ingestion, transformation, and analysis.

Code Example: Modular Workflow

python

```python
def ingest_data():
    return ["data1", "data2"]

def transform_data(data):
    return [d.upper() for d in data]

def analyze_data(data):
    print("Analyzed data:", data)

# Execute workflow
data = ingest_data()
transformed_data = transform_data(data)
analyze_data(transformed_data)
```

16.4.2 Implementing Load Balancing and Redundancy

1. Benefits:

- Prevents system overload.
- Ensures high availability.

2. **Tools:**
    - **NGINX:** For HTTP load balancing.
    - **Kubernetes:** Distributes workloads across pods.

Code Example: Load Balancing with NGINX

nginx

```
http {
  upstream backend {
    server backend1.example.com;
    server backend2.example.com;
  }

  server {
    location / {
      proxy_pass http://backend;
    }
  }
}
```

16.5 Case Studies

16.5.1 Scaling AutoGen for a Growing E-commerce Platform

Scenario: An e-commerce platform used AutoGen to automate customer support and inventory management.

Outcome:

- Scaled workflows to handle peak shopping seasons.

- Improved customer satisfaction by 25%.

16.5.2 Optimizing Costs for a SaaS Business with AutoGen

Scenario: A SaaS company optimized its AutoGen workflows by transitioning to serverless architectures.

Outcome:

- Reduced costs by 40%.
- Achieved faster deployment cycles.

16.6 Hands-On Project

16.6.1 Scaling an AI-Powered Workflow Automation System

Objective: Scale an AutoGen system to handle increasing workloads while maintaining efficiency.

Steps:

1. Implement auto-scaling.
2. Use load balancing for redundancy.
3. Monitor system performance and costs.

Code Example: Scaling with Kubernetes

```yaml
apiVersion: apps/v1
kind: Deployment
metadata:
  name: autogen-deployment
spec:
  replicas: 3
```

```
  template:
    spec:
      containers:
      - name: autogen-app
        image: autogen-image
```

16.7 Practice Problems and Quizzes

16.7.1 Mastering System Scaling and Optimization

Problem: Design a workflow that scales dynamically based on input data size.

16.7.2 Interactive Quizzes

Question: Which tool is best suited for load balancing in AutoGen systems?

1. Docker
2. Kubernetes
3. Apache Spark

Answer: 2. Kubernetes.

16.8 End-of-Chapter Summaries

16.8.1 Key Takeaways

- Scalability ensures AutoGen systems handle growing demands efficiently.
- Cost optimization strategies reduce operational expenses without compromising performance.

16.8.2 Quick Reference Guides

Task	Tool/Library	Key Functionality
Auto-Scaling	AWS Lambda, Kubernetes	Dynamically allocate resources.
Workflow Optimization	Python, multiprocessing	Enhance processing efficiency.

16.9 Templates and Tools

16.9.1 Workflow Templates

Template for Scaling AutoGen Systems:

1. Monitor workloads and costs.
2. Implement auto-scaling for compute resources.
3. Optimize workflows using parallel processing.

16.9.2 Scripts and Snippets

Reusable Script for Monitoring System Performance:

python

```python
import psutil

# Monitor CPU and memory usage
cpu_usage = psutil.cpu_percent()
memory_usage = psutil.virtual_memory().percent
print(f"CPU Usage: {cpu_usage}%, Memory Usage: {memory_usage}%")
```

This chapter explored strategies for scaling and optimizing AutoGen systems, focusing on infrastructure, performance, and cost management. With practical examples, tools, and case studies, readers can build scalable and efficient systems that meet the demands of modern workflows.

Chapter 17: Security and Compliance in AutoGen

As AutoGen systems become integral to workflows across industries, ensuring robust security and compliance is crucial. This chapter focuses on embedding security in AutoGen workflows, adhering to regulatory requirements, and mitigating potential AI threats. It provides actionable strategies, real-world examples, and hands-on projects to help readers build secure and compliant AutoGen systems.

17.1 Embedding Security in AutoGen Workflows

17.1.1 Securing Data Pipelines and AI Models

1. Importance of Securing Data Pipelines:

- Data pipelines are vulnerable to breaches during ingestion, transformation, and storage.
- Encryption and secure transmission protocols are essential.

2. Best Practices:

- **Encryption:** Use protocols like TLS for data in transit and AES for data at rest.
- **Data Masking:** Obfuscate sensitive data fields to prevent unauthorized access.
- **Monitoring:** Continuously track data flow to identify anomalies.

Code Example: Securing Data Transmission with Python

python

```python
from cryptography.fernet import Fernet

# Generate encryption key
key = Fernet.generate_key()
cipher_suite = Fernet(key)

# Encrypt data
data = "Sensitive Information".encode()
encrypted_data = cipher_suite.encrypt(data)
print("Encrypted Data:", encrypted_data)

# Decrypt data
decrypted_data = cipher_suite.decrypt(encrypted_data)
print("Decrypted Data:", decrypted_data.decode())
```

3. Securing AI Models:

- Restrict access to trained models using authentication.
- Encrypt model files during storage.
- Monitor for unauthorized usage of APIs exposing the model.

17.1.2 Implementing Access Controls and Authentication

1. Role-Based Access Control (RBAC):

- Assign permissions based on user roles (e.g., admin, developer, viewer).
- Prevent unauthorized modifications to AutoGen workflows.

2. Authentication Mechanisms:

- Use OAuth 2.0 for secure API authentication.
- Implement multi-factor authentication (MFA) for sensitive operations.

Code Example: Implementing API Authentication with Flask

python

```python
from flask import Flask, request, jsonify
from functools import wraps

app = Flask(__name__)

# Mock API key
API_KEY = "secret_key"

# Authentication decorator
def authenticate(f):
    @wraps(f)
    def decorated_function(*args, **kwargs):
        key = request.headers.get('API-Key')
        if key != API_KEY:
            return jsonify({"message": "Unauthorized"}), 403
        return f(*args, **kwargs)
    return decorated_function

@app.route('/secure-data', methods=['GET'])
@authenticate
def secure_data():
    return jsonify({"data": "Secure Content"})

if __name__ == "__main__":
    app.run(debug=True)
```

17.2 Meeting Compliance Requirements

17.2.1 Understanding Industry-Specific Regulations

1. Key Regulations by Industry:

- **Finance:** GDPR, PCI DSS.
- **Healthcare:** HIPAA, HITECH.
- **Technology:** CCPA, SOC 2.

2. **Importance:**
- Non-compliance can lead to heavy fines and reputational damage.
- Ensures trust with customers and stakeholders.

17.2.2 Automating Compliance Monitoring and Reporting

1. **Automation Use Cases:**
- Monitor access logs for unauthorized activity.
- Generate compliance reports periodically.

2. **Tools for Automation:**
- **AWS Audit Manager:** Automates evidence collection for compliance.
- **Splunk:** Provides real-time insights and reporting.

Code Example: Generating Audit Logs

python

```python
import logging

# Configure logging
logging.basicConfig(filename='audit.log', level=logging.INFO)

def log_access(user, action):
    logging.info(f"User: {user}, Action: {action}")

# Log actions
```

```
log_access("admin", "Updated workflow")
log_access("user1", "Accessed data pipeline")
```

17.3 Protecting Against AI Threats

17.3.1 Mitigating Risks of Adversarial Attacks

1. What Are Adversarial Attacks?

- Inputs crafted to deceive AI models into making incorrect predictions.
- Common in image recognition and NLP applications.

2. Mitigation Strategies:

- Use adversarial training to harden models.
- Employ robust preprocessing to sanitize inputs.
- Monitor predictions for anomalies.

Code Example: Detecting Anomalous Inputs

python

```python
import numpy as np

def detect_anomalies(input_data):
    threshold = 0.9  # Confidence threshold
    confidence = np.random.rand()  # Mock confidence score
    if confidence < threshold:
        return "Potential adversarial input detected"
    return "Input is valid"

# Example usage
result = detect_anomalies("input_data")
print(result)
```

17.3.2 Ensuring Model Integrity and Reliability

1. Threats to Model Integrity:

- Model theft: Unauthorized access to model files.
- Poisoning attacks: Corruption of training data.

2. Countermeasures:

- Encrypt models and their storage.
- Validate training datasets for consistency.

17.4 Case Studies

17.4.1 Automating Compliance Reporting for Financial Institutions

Scenario: A bank used AutoGen to automate its GDPR compliance reporting by monitoring access logs and generating audit trails.

Outcome:

- Reduced manual effort by 50%.
- Improved response time for audits.

17.4.2 Enhancing Security in AI-Powered Customer Support Systems

Scenario: An e-commerce platform implemented AutoGen to secure its AI-powered chatbot by encrypting sensitive customer data and using RBAC for model access.

Outcome:

- Improved customer trust.
- Prevented data breaches during interactions.

17.5 Hands-On Project

17.5.1 Implementing Security Best Practices in an AutoGen Workflow

Objective: Secure an AutoGen workflow that processes sensitive customer data, ensuring encryption and controlled access.

Steps:

1. Encrypt data during ingestion.
2. Authenticate access to workflows.
3. Log all actions for audit purposes.

Code Example: Secure Workflow Implementation

python

```python
def secure_workflow(data, api_key):
    # Step 1: Authenticate
    if api_key != "secure_key":
        return "Unauthorized Access"

    # Step 2: Encrypt Data
    encrypted_data = cipher_suite.encrypt(data.encode())

    # Step 3: Log Action
    log_access("user", "Processed encrypted data")
    return encrypted_data

# Usage
data = "Customer Information"
api_key = "secure_key"
print("Result:", secure_workflow(data, api_key))
```

17.6 Practice Problems and Quizzes

17.6.1 Ensuring Security and Compliance in AutoGen Systems

Problem: Write a script to monitor suspicious API usage patterns in an AutoGen system.

17.6.2 Interactive Quizzes

Question: Which technique is most effective for mitigating adversarial attacks?

1. Data masking.
2. Adversarial training.
3. RBAC.

Answer: 2. Adversarial training.

17.7 End-of-Chapter Summaries

17.7.1 Key Takeaways

- Securing AutoGen workflows involves encrypting data, implementing access controls, and monitoring actions.
- Compliance automation reduces manual overhead and ensures adherence to industry regulations.

17.7.2 Quick Reference Guides

Task	Tool/Library	Key Functionality
Data Encryption	Python Cryptography	Secure data at rest and in transit.

Task	Tool/Library	Key Functionality
Compliance Monitoring	AWS Audit Manager	Automates evidence collection.

17.8 Templates and Tools

17.8.1 Workflow Templates

Template for Secure Workflows:

1. Authenticate access requests.
2. Encrypt data during processing.
3. Log actions for compliance reporting.

17.8.2 Scripts and Snippets

Reusable Script for Role-Based Access Control:

python

```python
def check_access(user_role, resource):
    permissions = {
        "admin": ["read", "write", "delete"],
        "user": ["read", "write"],
        "viewer": ["read"]
    }
    return permissions.get(user_role, [])

# Example usage
role = "user"
action = "write"
if action in check_access(role, "workflow"):
    print("Access granted")
```

```
else:
    print("Access denied")
```

This chapter provided a comprehensive guide to securing and ensuring compliance in AutoGen workflows. With practical strategies, case studies, and hands-on projects, readers can build robust systems that adhere to industry standards while mitigating potential threats.

Chapter 18: Monitoring and Observability in AutoGen Systems

Monitoring and observability are essential components of maintaining efficient, reliable, and scalable AutoGen systems. Proper observability ensures that developers and operators can gain insights into system performance, detect issues proactively, and respond to incidents promptly. This chapter explores the best practices, tools, and strategies for implementing observability in AutoGen systems, supported by real-world case studies, hands-on projects, and actionable templates.

18.1 Best Practices for Observability

18.1.1 Key Metrics and Indicators to Monitor

1. Importance of Observability Metrics:

- Metrics enable real-time insights into system performance and behavior.
- Monitoring these indicators helps identify bottlenecks and potential issues before they impact workflows.

2. Key Metrics for AutoGen Systems:

- **Latency:** Time taken to complete a workflow or task.
- **Throughput:** Number of workflows processed in a given time frame.
- **Error Rates:** Frequency of failed tasks or processes.
- **Resource Utilization:** CPU, memory, and network usage.
- **Model Performance:** Metrics like accuracy, precision, and recall for AI models.

Example Table: Metrics and Their Relevance

Metric	Purpose	Monitoring Tool
Latency	Detect workflow delays	Prometheus, Grafana
Throughput	Measure system capacity	ELK Stack
Error Rates	Identify process failures	Sentry
Resource Utilization	Prevent resource overuse	AWS CloudWatch, Datadog
Model Accuracy	Monitor AI prediction quality	Custom Metrics

18.1.2 Setting Up Monitoring Dashboards

1. Why Dashboards Matter:

- Dashboards centralize metrics and logs for easy visualization.
- Provide quick insights into system health and performance trends.

2. Tools for Dashboard Creation:

- **Grafana:** A powerful, open-source observability tool.
- **Kibana:** Works with Elasticsearch for log visualization.
- **AWS CloudWatch:** Comprehensive monitoring for cloud-based systems.

Code Example: Setting Up a Grafana Dashboard

bash

```
# Step 1: Install Grafana
sudo apt-get install -y grafana

# Step 2: Configure data source
```

```
# Connect Grafana to Prometheus or another data source.

# Step 3: Create metrics dashboard
# Use Grafana's web interface to add panels and configure metrics for latency, error rates, etc.
```

18.2 Logging and Analytics

18.2.1 Implementing Comprehensive Logging Strategies

1. Importance of Logging:

- Logs capture detailed information about system activities and errors.
- Essential for debugging and forensic analysis during incidents.

2. Best Practices for Logging:

- Include timestamps, severity levels, and context in logs.
- Use structured logging formats like JSON for compatibility with analytics tools.
- Rotate logs to prevent storage overflows.

Code Example: Python Logging Setup

python

```python
import logging

# Configure logging
logging.basicConfig(
    filename='autogen_system.log',
    level=logging.INFO,
    format='%(asctime)s - %(levelname)s - %(message)s'
)
```

```
# Log events
logging.info("Workflow started")
logging.error("Error in processing data")
```

18.2.2 Leveraging Analytics for Performance Insights

1. Benefits of Analytics:

- Identify trends and patterns over time.
- Correlate metrics to uncover root causes of issues.

2. Tools for Log Analytics:

- **Elasticsearch + Kibana (ELK Stack):** Analyze and visualize logs.
- **Splunk:** Advanced log analytics and reporting.

Example Workflow for Log Analytics:

1. Collect logs from AutoGen workflows.
2. Ingest logs into Elasticsearch for indexing.
3. Visualize log trends using Kibana dashboards.

18.3 Automated Alerting and Incident Response

18.3.1 Setting Up Alerts for Critical Events

1. Benefits of Alerts:

- Notify teams about potential issues in real-time.
- Enable faster response times to incidents.

2. Setting Up Alerts:

- Define thresholds for critical metrics (e.g., error rate > 5%).
- Use alerting tools like PagerDuty, Slack, or email notifications.

Code Example: Configuring Alerts in Prometheus

yaml

```
groups:
  - name: auto-gen-alerts
    rules:
      - alert: HighErrorRate
        expr: rate(errors_total[5m]) > 0.05
        for: 1m
        labels:
          severity: critical
        annotations:
          summary: "High error rate detected in AutoGen workflows"
```

18.3.2 Automating Incident Management Workflows

1. Automating Responses:

- Use tools like Rundeck or Zapier to trigger automated responses to alerts.
- Automate tasks such as restarting workflows, scaling resources, or notifying stakeholders.

Code Example: Automating Workflow Restart

python

```
import subprocess

def restart_workflow(workflow_id):
    try:
```

```
        subprocess.run(["systemctl", "restart", workflow_id], check=True)
        print(f"Workflow {workflow_id} restarted successfully.")
    except subprocess.CalledProcessError as e:
        print(f"Failed to restart workflow: {e}")

# Trigger workflow restart
restart_workflow("autogen-workflow")
```

18.4 Case Studies

18.4.1 Monitoring AutoGen Workflows in a Healthcare Setting

Scenario: A hospital used AutoGen to automate patient record processing. Monitoring ensured compliance with HIPAA regulations and uninterrupted performance.

Outcome:

- Reduced system downtime by 30%.
- Ensured faster response times for workflow errors.

18.4.2 Implementing Observability for an AI-Powered Marketing Platform

Scenario: A marketing platform leveraged observability tools to monitor campaign performance and resource utilization.

Outcome:

- Identified bottlenecks in high-traffic scenarios.
- Improved campaign processing speeds by 20%.

18.5 Hands-On Project

18.5.1 Building an Observability Dashboard for an AutoGen System

Objective: Develop a real-time monitoring dashboard for an AutoGen system using Grafana.

Steps:

1. Set up Prometheus as the data source.
2. Configure AutoGen workflows to export metrics to Prometheus.
3. Build Grafana panels for latency, error rates, and resource utilization.

Code Example: Exporting Metrics for Monitoring

python

```python
from prometheus_client import start_http_server, Counter

# Define metrics
workflow_counter = Counter("workflow_requests_total", "Total workflow requests")

# Increment counter
def process_workflow():
    workflow_counter.inc()
    # Simulate workflow processing
    print("Processing workflow...")

# Start metrics server
start_http_server(8000)
process_workflow()
```

18.6 Practice Problems and Quizzes

18.6.1 Enhancing System Monitoring and Observability

Problem: Write a Python script to calculate error rates from log data and generate alerts if the rate exceeds a threshold.

18.6.2 Interactive Quizzes

Question: Which tool is best suited for visualizing log data?

1. Grafana
2. Kibana
3. Prometheus

Answer: 2. Kibana.

18.7 End-of-Chapter Summaries

18.7.1 Key Takeaways

- Monitoring key metrics and implementing comprehensive logging strategies enhance observability.
- Automated alerts and dashboards ensure real-time insights into system performance.

18.7.2 Quick Reference Guides

Task	Tool/Library	Key Functionality
Real-Time Monitoring	Prometheus, Grafana	Collect and visualize metrics.
Log Analytics	ELK Stack, Splunk	Analyze system logs.

18.8 Templates and Tools

18.8.1 Workflow Templates

Template for Observability:

1. Export metrics and logs from workflows.
2. Visualize data in dashboards.
3. Configure alerts for critical events.

18.8.2 Scripts and Snippets

Reusable Script for Log Analysis:

python

```python
def analyze_logs(log_file):
    with open(log_file, "r") as f:
        errors = [line for line in f if "ERROR" in line]
    return len(errors)

# Usage
error_count = analyze_logs("autogen_system.log")
print("Total Errors:", error_count)
```

This chapter covered the importance of monitoring and observability in AutoGen systems. By leveraging the best practices, tools, and workflows outlined here, developers can ensure reliable and efficient system operations while minimizing downtime and performance issues.

Chapter 19: Advanced AutoGen Techniques and Customizations

As workflows become more complex, leveraging advanced AutoGen techniques and customizations can unlock the full potential of automation systems. This chapter delves into fine-tuning large language models (LLMs), developing custom AI agents, and integrating machine learning pipelines into workflow automation. Readers will explore best practices, practical examples, and hands-on projects to enhance their AutoGen systems.

19.1 Fine-Tuning Large Language Models

19.1.1 Techniques for Customizing AI Models

1. What is Fine-Tuning?

- Fine-tuning involves adapting a pre-trained large language model to specific tasks or datasets by training it further on domain-specific data.

2. Benefits of Fine-Tuning:

- Improves accuracy for niche applications.
- Reduces irrelevant outputs by focusing on domain-specific knowledge.
- Customizes models for unique use cases, such as medical or legal documentation.

3. Techniques for Fine-Tuning:

- **Data Preparation:**
    - Curate high-quality, domain-specific datasets.
    - Clean and preprocess data to remove noise and inconsistencies.

- **Training Strategies:**
    - Use low learning rates to preserve general knowledge in the pre-trained model.
    - Employ transfer learning to build on existing model capabilities.
- **Tools:**
    - Hugging Face Transformers.
    - OpenAI's fine-tuning APIs.

Code Example: Fine-Tuning GPT Using Hugging Face

python

```python
from transformers import GPT2Tokenizer, GPT2LMHeadModel, Trainer, TrainingArguments
from datasets import load_dataset

# Load dataset and model
dataset = load_dataset("your_dataset")
tokenizer = GPT2Tokenizer.from_pretrained("gpt2")
model = GPT2LMHeadModel.from_pretrained("gpt2")

# Tokenize data
def preprocess(data):
    return tokenizer(data["text"], truncation=True, padding="max_length", max_length=128)

dataset = dataset.map(preprocess, batched=True)

# Fine-tuning
training_args = TrainingArguments(
    output_dir="./results",
    num_train_epochs=3,
```

```
    per_device_train_batch_size=4,
    save_steps=10_000,
    save_total_limit=2,
)
trainer = Trainer(
    model=model,
    args=training_args,
    train_dataset=dataset["train"],
    eval_dataset=dataset["validation"],
)
trainer.train()
```

19.1.2 Best Practices for Model Training and Deployment

1. Data Considerations:

- Ensure datasets are balanced and representative.
- Avoid overfitting by including diverse examples.

2. Deployment Tips:

- Optimize models for inference using techniques like quantization.
- Use cloud platforms such as AWS SageMaker or Azure ML for scalable deployments.

19.2 Developing Custom AI Agents

19.2.1 Designing Specialized Agents for Specific Tasks

1. Characteristics of Specialized Agents:

- Focus on a defined task or domain, such as financial analysis or customer service.
- Operate autonomously within their scope, using task-specific logic.

2. Key Design Steps:

- Define the agent's objective and task boundaries.
- Design interaction protocols with other agents or workflows.

Code Example: Specialized Agent for Customer Support

python

```python
class CustomerSupportAgent:
    def __init__(self):
        self.responses = {
            "billing": "I can assist with billing inquiries.",
            "technical": "Let me connect you to technical support.",
        }

    def handle_query(self, query):
        for keyword in self.responses:
            if keyword in query.lower():
                return self.responses[keyword]
        return "I'm sorry, I don't understand the query."

agent = CustomerSupportAgent()
print(agent.handle_query("I have a billing issue."))
```

19.2.2 Implementing Multi-Agent Coordination Strategies

1. What is Multi-Agent Coordination?

- Multi-agent systems involve several agents working together to achieve shared objectives.

2. Coordination Strategies:

- **Task Allocation:** Distribute tasks based on agent capabilities.

- **Communication Protocols:** Use message-passing mechanisms to enable agent interaction.
- **Conflict Resolution:** Define rules to resolve disputes between agents.

Code Example: Agent Communication Using Python

python

```
class Agent:
    def __init__(self, name):
        self.name = name

    def communicate(self, message):
        print(f"{self.name} received message: {message}")

# Define agents
agent1 = Agent("Agent 1")
agent2 = Agent("Agent 2")

# Simulate communication
agent1.communicate("Hello from Agent 2!")
```

19.3 Enhancing AutoGen with Machine Learning Pipelines

19.3.1 Integrating ML Models into Workflow Automation

1. Key Components of an ML Pipeline:
- **Data Ingestion:** Extract and preprocess data.
- **Model Training:** Train models using historical data.
- **Inference:** Apply trained models to make predictions.

2. Integration Techniques:

- Use RESTful APIs to connect ML models to AutoGen workflows.
- Implement batch processing for large datasets.

Code Example: Connecting ML Model to Workflow

python

```
from flask import Flask, request, jsonify
import pickle

# Load trained model
with open("model.pkl", "rb") as f:
    model = pickle.load(f)

# Define API
app = Flask(__name__)

@app.route("/predict", methods=["POST"])
def predict():
    data = request.json["data"]
    prediction = model.predict([data])
    return jsonify({"prediction": prediction[0]})

app.run(port=5000)
```

19.3.2 Automating Model Training and Deployment

1. Automation Tools:
- MLFlow for end-to-end model lifecycle management.
- Kubeflow for orchestrating ML pipelines.

2. Benefits:
- Reduces manual intervention in retraining and deployment.

- Ensures models remain up-to-date with changing data.

19.4 Case Studies

19.4.1 Customizing AI Models for Personalized Customer Interactions

Scenario: A retail company fine-tuned GPT to create personalized product recommendations for customers.

Outcome:

- Increased customer engagement by 25%.
- Reduced bounce rates on e-commerce platforms.

19.4.2 Developing Specialized Agents for Financial Analysis

Scenario: A financial firm developed custom agents for analyzing market trends and providing investment insights.

Outcome:

- Reduced manual analysis time by 40%.
- Delivered more accurate and timely insights.

19.5 Hands-On Project

19.5.1 Fine-Tuning an LLM for a Specific Automation Task

Objective: Fine-tune GPT to automate summarization of customer support tickets.

Steps:

1. Collect and preprocess ticket data.

2. Fine-tune GPT on the dataset using Hugging Face.
3. Deploy the model as a REST API for integration.

Code Example: Summarization Fine-Tuning *(Refer to Section 19.1.1 for code.)*

19.6 Practice Problems and Quizzes

19.6.1 Mastering Advanced Techniques and Customizations

Problem: Write a script to train a custom AI agent for detecting fraud in transaction data.

19.6.2 Interactive Quizzes

Question: Which tool is best suited for managing the ML lifecycle?

1. Hugging Face
2. MLFlow
3. Flask

Answer: 2. MLFlow.

19.7 End-of-Chapter Summaries

19.7.1 Key Takeaways

- Fine-tuning enhances the performance of pre-trained models for niche applications.
- Custom agents and ML pipelines unlock the potential for advanced workflow automation.

19.7.2 Quick Reference Guides

Task	Tool/Library	Key Functionality
Model Fine-Tuning	Hugging Face, PyTorch	Customize AI models.
Multi-Agent Coordination	Custom Python Scripts	Enable agent communication.

19.8 Templates and Tools

19.8.1 Workflow Templates

Template for Advanced AutoGen Workflow:

1. Fine-tune AI models.
2. Design custom agents for tasks.
3. Integrate models into workflows.

19.8.2 Scripts and Snippets

Reusable Snippet for API Integration:

python

```python
import requests

data = {"data": "Sample input"}
response = requests.post("http://localhost:5000/predict", json=data)
print("Prediction:", response.json())
```

This chapter introduced advanced techniques for fine-tuning LLMs, developing custom agents, and integrating machine learning pipelines into AutoGen workflows. With detailed case studies, examples, and hands-on projects, readers are equipped to enhance and customize their automation systems for complex and specialized use cases.

Part IV: Real-World Applications and Case Studies

Chapter 20: AutoGen in Healthcare

Healthcare systems worldwide are increasingly adopting automation and AI-driven solutions to improve patient care, streamline workflows, and enhance decision-making. AutoGen plays a critical role in healthcare by automating repetitive tasks, improving data accuracy, and supporting clinical diagnostics. This chapter explores real-world applications, case studies, and hands-on projects to demonstrate the transformative potential of AutoGen in healthcare.

20.1 Automating Patient Data Management

20.1.1 Streamlining Electronic Health Records (EHR) Systems

1. Challenges in EHR Management:

- Manual data entry leads to errors and inefficiencies.
- Lack of interoperability between systems hinders information sharing.
- Time-consuming administrative tasks reduce focus on patient care.

2. AutoGen Solutions:

- **Automated Data Entry:** Extract and input patient information from forms using Natural Language Processing (NLP).
- **Interoperability:** Facilitate seamless data exchange between EHR systems using APIs.

Code Example: Automating Data Extraction from Patient Forms

python

```python
import pytesseract
from PIL import Image

# Extract text from patient form
image = Image.open("patient_form.png")
text = pytesseract.image_to_string(image)
print("Extracted Text:", text)

# Simulate structured data insertion
patient_data = {"name": "John Doe", "age": 30, "condition": "Diabetes"}
print("Patient Data:", patient_data)
```

20.1.2 Enhancing Data Accuracy and Accessibility

1. Ensuring Accuracy:

- Use AutoGen to cross-validate data against existing records.
- Flag discrepancies for manual review.

2. Improving Accessibility:

- Implement searchable databases with AI-powered queries.
- Enable voice-activated data retrieval for healthcare professionals.

Code Example: AI-Powered Data Search

python

```python
from whoosh.index import create_in
from whoosh.fields import Schema, TEXT

# Create a searchable schema
schema = Schema(name=TEXT, condition=TEXT)
index = create_in("indexdir", schema)
```

```python
# Add patient data
writer = index.writer()
writer.add_document(name="John Doe", condition="Diabetes")
writer.add_document(name="Jane Smith", condition="Hypertension")
writer.commit()

# Search patient records
from whoosh.qparser import QueryParser
with index.searcher() as searcher:
    query = QueryParser("condition", index.schema).parse("Diabetes")
    results = searcher.search(query)
    for result in results:
        print("Found:", result["name"])
```

20.2 AI-Driven Diagnostics and Decision Support

20.2.1 Automating Diagnostic Processes

1. Automating Routine Diagnostics:

- Use AI models to analyze medical images such as X-rays or MRIs.
- Automate lab test result interpretation for common conditions.

2. Benefits:

- Reduces diagnostic errors.
- Speeds up the diagnostic process.

Code Example: Image Analysis with AI

python

```python
from tensorflow.keras.models import load_model
from tensorflow.keras.preprocessing.image import load_img, img_to_array

# Load pre-trained model
model = load_model("medical_image_model.h5")

# Analyze X-ray image
image = load_img("chest_xray.png", target_size=(224, 224))
image_array = img_to_array(image).reshape(1, 224, 224, 3)
prediction = model.predict(image_array)
print("Prediction:", "Pneumonia" if prediction[0] > 0.5 else "Normal")
```

20.2.2 Supporting Clinical Decision-Making with AI

1. Role of AI in Decision Support:

- Provide treatment recommendations based on patient history and symptoms.
- Predict outcomes and risks using machine learning models.

2. Tools and Frameworks:

- TensorFlow, PyTorch for model development.
- IBM Watson for advanced clinical decision support.

Code Example: Predicting Patient Risk

python

```python
from sklearn.ensemble import RandomForestClassifier
import numpy as np

# Simulate patient data
patient_features = np.array([[45, 1, 1]])  # [Age, Diabetes (Yes=1), Hypertension (Yes=1)]
```

```
# Train model (mock example)
model = RandomForestClassifier()
X_train = [[30, 0, 1], [50, 1, 1], [40, 0, 0]]
y_train = [0, 1, 0]  # [Low Risk, High Risk, Low Risk]
model.fit(X_train, y_train)

# Predict risk
risk = model.predict(patient_features)
print("Risk Level:", "High" if risk[0] == 1 else "Low")
```

20.3 Case Studies

20.3.1 Implementing AutoGen for Telemedicine Services

Scenario: A telemedicine provider used AutoGen to automate appointment scheduling, patient triage, and follow-up reminders.

Outcome:

- Increased patient engagement by 40%.
- Reduced administrative workload for healthcare staff.

20.3.2 Enhancing Healthcare Analytics with AI

Scenario: A hospital leveraged AutoGen for real-time analysis of patient data to identify trends in disease outbreaks.

Outcome:

- Improved response times for handling infectious disease cases.
- Enabled proactive resource allocation.

20.4 Hands-On Project

20.4.1 Developing an AI-Powered Patient Data Management System

Objective: Build a system to automate the ingestion, processing, and querying of patient data.

Steps:

1. Extract patient data from scanned forms using OCR.
2. Store data in a searchable database.
3. Develop an interface for querying patient records.

Code Example: Combining OCR and Search *(Refer to Sections 20.1.1 and 20.1.2 for code snippets.)*

20.5 Practice Problems and Quizzes

20.5.1 Applying AutoGen in Healthcare Scenarios

Problem: Write a Python script to predict the likelihood of a patient developing a chronic condition based on lifestyle data.

20.5.2 Interactive Quizzes

Question: Which AutoGen application is best suited for improving EHR systems?

1. AI-powered data search.
2. Automated image analysis.
3. Predictive risk modeling.

Answer: 1. AI-powered data search.

20.6 End-of-Chapter Summaries

20.6.1 Key Takeaways

- AutoGen enhances data management, diagnostics, and decision-making in healthcare.
- Real-world applications demonstrate its potential to improve efficiency and patient outcomes.

20.6.2 Quick Reference Guides

Task	Tool/Library	Key Functionality
Data Extraction	Tesseract OCR	Extracts text from scanned forms.
Risk Prediction	Scikit-Learn	Analyzes patient data for risks.

20.7 Templates and Tools

20.7.1 Workflow Templates

Template for Patient Data Management:

1. Ingest data using OCR.
2. Validate and store data in a database.
3. Query data using an AI-powered search tool.

20.7.2 Scripts and Snippets

Reusable Script for Patient Data Querying:

python

```
def search_patient_data(records, query):
    return [record for record in records if query.lower() in record["condition"].lower()]
```

```python
# Example data
patient_records = [
    {"name": "John Doe", "condition": "Diabetes"},
    {"name": "Jane Smith", "condition": "Hypertension"},
]

# Query patient data
results = search_patient_data(patient_records, "Diabetes")
print("Matching Records:", results)
```

AutoGen's potential in healthcare is transformative, from automating routine tasks to supporting advanced diagnostics and analytics. With practical tools, templates, and real-world insights, this chapter equips readers to harness AutoGen's capabilities to improve patient care and operational efficiency.

Chapter 21: AutoGen in Finance

The finance sector is increasingly leveraging AutoGen technologies to automate routine tasks, enhance decision-making, and ensure compliance. From streamlining financial reporting to risk management and fraud detection, AutoGen provides tools to make financial systems more efficient, accurate, and secure. This chapter explores the key applications of AutoGen in finance, supported by case studies, hands-on projects, and actionable tools.

21.1 Automating Financial Reporting and Compliance

21.1.1 Streamlining Financial Statements and Reports

1. Challenges in Financial Reporting:

- Time-consuming data collection and consolidation processes.
- Risk of human errors in calculations and formatting.
- Complexities in generating customized reports for stakeholders.

2. AutoGen Solutions:

- **Automated Report Generation:** Generate financial statements such as income statements, balance sheets, and cash flow statements.
- **Data Consolidation:** Aggregate data from multiple sources using APIs and ETL (Extract, Transform, Load) pipelines.
- **Dynamic Formatting:** Use AI to create visually appealing, customized reports.

Code Example: Generating Financial Reports

python

```python
import pandas as pd

# Sample financial data
data = {
    "Category": ["Revenue", "Expenses", "Profit"],
    "Amount": [100000, 75000, 25000]
}

# Create a DataFrame
df = pd.DataFrame(data)

# Generate financial report
def generate_report(dataframe):
    report = f"Financial Report:\n"
    for index, row in dataframe.iterrows():
        report += f"{row['Category']}: ${row['Amount']}\n"
    return report

print(generate_report(df))
```

21.1.2 Ensuring Compliance with Financial Regulations

1. Key Regulations:

- **SOX (Sarbanes-Oxley Act):** Requires accurate financial reporting and internal controls.
- **AML (Anti-Money Laundering) Regulations:** Enforces monitoring and reporting of suspicious financial activities.
- **IFRS/GAAP:** Standardizes financial reporting practices globally.

2. AutoGen Tools for Compliance:

- Automate regulatory checks using rule-based engines.
- Generate compliance reports with audit trails for transparency.

Code Example: Automating Compliance Checks

python

```python
def check_compliance(transaction):
    rules = {
        "AML_Limit": 10000,  # Transactions above this require reporting
        "Suspicious_Countries": ["CountryA", "CountryB"]
    }

    if transaction["amount"] > rules["AML_Limit"]:
        return f"Transaction flagged for AML: {transaction}"
    if transaction["country"] in rules["Suspicious_Countries"]:
        return f"Transaction flagged for country monitoring: {transaction}"
    return "Transaction compliant"

# Example transaction
transaction = {"amount": 12000, "country": "CountryA"}
print(check_compliance(transaction))
```

21.2 AI for Risk Management and Fraud Detection

21.2.1 Automating Risk Assessment Processes

1. AutoGen in Risk Management:

- Identify and quantify risks using AI models.

- Automate the creation of risk profiles for investment portfolios.

2. Key Techniques:
- Monte Carlo simulations for market risk analysis.
- Predictive analytics for credit risk assessment.

Code Example: Risk Assessment with Python

python

```python
import numpy as np

# Simulate portfolio returns
np.random.seed(42)
portfolio_returns = np.random.normal(0.01, 0.05, 1000)

# Calculate Value at Risk (VaR)
VaR_95 = np.percentile(portfolio_returns, 5)
print(f"95% Value at Risk: {VaR_95:.2%}")
```

21.2.2 Enhancing Fraud Detection with AI Models

1. Common Fraud Scenarios:
- Unusual transaction patterns.
- Identity theft and account takeover.
- Fake claims in insurance.

2. AI-Based Detection:
- Use anomaly detection to flag unusual activities.
- Train supervised models to classify fraudulent transactions.

Code Example: Fraud Detection with Scikit-Learn

python

```python
from sklearn.ensemble import IsolationForest

# Sample transaction data
transactions = [[100, 1], [200, 1], [5000, 0], [150, 1], [10000, 0]]  # [Amount, Normal(1)/Fraud(0)]

# Train Isolation Forest
clf = IsolationForest(random_state=42)
clf.fit(transactions)

# Predict anomalies
anomalies = clf.predict([[6000, 1]])  # Predict for a new transaction
print("Fraudulent" if anomalies[0] == -1 else "Normal")
```

21.3 Case Studies

21.3.1 Implementing AutoGen for Automated Trading Systems

Scenario: A trading firm implemented AutoGen to automate stock trading based on predefined algorithms and market conditions.

Outcome:

- Improved trade execution speed by 40%.
- Reduced human errors in trading strategies.

21.3.2 Enhancing Fraud Detection in Banking with AI

Scenario: A bank used AutoGen to monitor customer transactions for suspicious activities, leveraging anomaly detection algorithms.

Outcome:

- Reduced false positives in fraud detection by 25%.

- Improved customer trust through proactive fraud prevention.

21.4 Hands-On Project

21.4.1 Building an AI-Driven Financial Reporting Tool

Objective: Develop a tool to automate the generation of financial reports, integrating compliance checks and visualizations.

Steps:

1. Ingest financial data from spreadsheets or APIs.
2. Generate formatted reports using Python libraries.
3. Add compliance validation for each transaction.

Code Example: Combining Reporting and Compliance

python

```python
import matplotlib.pyplot as plt

# Generate financial report with chart
def generate_financial_chart(data):
    categories = data["Category"]
    amounts = data["Amount"]
    plt.bar(categories, amounts)
    plt.title("Financial Report")
    plt.ylabel("Amount ($)")
    plt.show()

generate_financial_chart(data)
```

21.5 Practice Problems and Quizzes

21.5.1 Leveraging AutoGen for Financial Applications

Problem: Write a Python script to identify the top 5 risky investment options from a portfolio dataset.

21.5.2 Interactive Quizzes

Question: Which AutoGen application is most effective for fraud detection?

1. Report automation.
2. Anomaly detection models.
3. Portfolio optimization.

Answer: 2. Anomaly detection models.

21.6 End-of-Chapter Summaries

21.6.1 Key Takeaways

- AutoGen improves financial reporting efficiency and accuracy.
- AI models enhance risk assessment and fraud detection capabilities.

21.6.2 Quick Reference Guides

Task	Tool/Library	Key Functionality
Report Generation	Pandas, Matplotlib	Automate report creation.
Fraud Detection	Scikit-Learn	Identify suspicious transactions.

21.7 Templates and Tools

21.7.1 Workflow Templates

Template for Financial Reporting:

1. Aggregate financial data.
2. Validate data for compliance.
3. Generate formatted reports and visualizations.

21.7.2 Scripts and Snippets

Reusable Snippet for Compliance Reporting:

python

```python
def generate_compliance_report(transactions):
    flagged = [check_compliance(tx) for tx in transactions]
    return [report for report in flagged if "flagged" in report]

# Example usage
transactions = [
    {"amount": 12000, "country": "CountryA"},
    {"amount": 500, "country": "CountryC"}
]
print(generate_compliance_report(transactions))
```

AutoGen's role in finance is transformative, offering automation solutions for reporting, compliance, risk management, and fraud detection. Through case studies, hands-on projects, and practical templates, this chapter equips readers to implement robust financial systems powered by AI and automation.

Chapter 22: AutoGen in E-commerce

E-commerce platforms increasingly leverage automation and AI technologies to enhance customer experiences, streamline operations, and optimize supply chains. AutoGen plays a pivotal role in automating repetitive tasks, providing personalized recommendations, and ensuring efficient inventory management. This chapter delves into these applications with case studies, hands-on projects, and actionable tools for implementing AutoGen in e-commerce workflows.

22.1 Personalizing Customer Experiences

22.1.1 Automating Product Recommendations

1. Importance of Product Recommendations:

- Drives customer engagement and sales by presenting relevant products.
- Increases average order value through cross-selling and upselling.

2. Techniques for Automating Recommendations:

- **Collaborative Filtering:** Suggest products based on user behavior and preferences.
- **Content-Based Filtering:** Match products to a user's previous interactions.
- **AI Models:** Leverage machine learning models for advanced personalization.

Code Example: Collaborative Filtering

python

```python
from sklearn.metrics.pairwise import cosine_similarity
import pandas as pd

# Sample user-item interaction matrix
data = {
    "User": ["Alice", "Bob", "Charlie"],
    "ProductA": [5, 4, 0],
    "ProductB": [4, 0, 3],
    "ProductC": [0, 3, 4],
}
df = pd.DataFrame(data).set_index("User")

# Calculate similarity
similarity = cosine_similarity(df.fillna(0))
print("User Similarity Matrix:")
print(similarity)

# Recommend products based on similar users
def recommend_products(user, user_similarity, df):
    user_index = df.index.tolist().index(user)
    similar_users = user_similarity[user_index].argsort()[::-1][1:]
    recommended_products = df.iloc[similar_users].mean().sort_values(ascending=False)
    return recommended_products.index.tolist()

recommendations = recommend_products("Alice", similarity, df)
print("Recommendations for Alice:", recommendations)
```

22.1.2 Enhancing Customer Journey with AI

1. Applications of AI in Customer Journeys:

- **Personalized Landing Pages:** Tailor website layouts based on customer preferences.
- **Dynamic Pricing:** Adjust product prices based on demand, competition, or user behavior.
- **AI Chatbots:** Provide real-time assistance for customer queries.

2. **Tools for Enhancing Customer Journeys:**
   - Google Analytics and AI platforms like TensorFlow for personalization.
   - CRM tools integrated with AutoGen workflows.

Example Use Case:

- A chatbot suggesting products based on customer inquiries:

python

```python
class Chatbot:
    def __init__(self):
        self.recommendations = {
            "shoes": ["Running Shoes", "Casual Sneakers"],
            "electronics": ["Smartphone", "Tablet"],
        }

    def respond(self, query):
        for category in self.recommendations:
            if category in query.lower():
                return f"I recommend: {', '.join(self.recommendations[category])}"
        return "How can I assist you further?"

bot = Chatbot()
print(bot.respond("I need new shoes."))
```

22.2 Inventory Management and Supply Chain Automation

22.2.1 Streamlining Inventory Tracking and Reordering

1. Challenges in Inventory Management:

- Overstocking leads to increased storage costs.
- Understocking results in lost sales and dissatisfied customers.

2. Solutions with AutoGen:

- **Real-Time Tracking:** Monitor inventory levels across multiple warehouses.
- **Automated Reordering:** Trigger orders when inventory reaches predefined thresholds.

Code Example: Reorder Point Calculation

python

```python
def calculate_reorder_point(daily_demand, lead_time, safety_stock):
    return (daily_demand * lead_time) + safety_stock

# Example inputs
daily_demand = 20
lead_time = 5  # days
safety_stock = 50

reorder_point = calculate_reorder_point(daily_demand, lead_time, safety_stock)
print(f"Reorder Point: {reorder_point} units")
```

22.2.2 Automating Supply Chain Processes with AI

1. **Applications in Supply Chains:**
   - **Route Optimization:** Use AI to find the most efficient delivery routes.
   - **Demand Forecasting:** Predict demand trends using machine learning.

2. **Benefits:**
   - Reduce delivery times and costs.
   - Optimize resource allocation across the supply chain.

Code Example: Predicting Demand with Linear Regression

python

```python
from sklearn.linear_model import LinearRegression
import numpy as np

# Historical sales data
days = np.array([1, 2, 3, 4, 5]).reshape(-1, 1)
sales = np.array([50, 60, 65, 80, 100])

# Train model
model = LinearRegression()
model.fit(days, sales)

# Predict future demand
future_days = np.array([6, 7, 8]).reshape(-1, 1)
predicted_sales = model.predict(future_days)
print("Predicted Sales:", predicted_sales)
```

22.3 Case Studies

22.3.1 Implementing AI-Powered Chatbots for Customer Support

Scenario: An online retailer deployed an AI-powered chatbot to handle common customer inquiries, such as order status and return policies.

Outcome:

- Resolved 80% of customer queries without human intervention.
- Improved customer satisfaction by 30%.

22.3.2 Enhancing Supply Chain Efficiency with AutoGen

Scenario: An e-commerce company automated its supply chain to dynamically adjust reorder quantities and optimize warehouse storage.

Outcome:

- Reduced stockouts by 40%.
- Lowered operational costs by 25%.

22.4 Hands-On Project

22.4.1 Developing an AI-Driven Product Recommendation Engine

Objective: Build a recommendation engine to suggest products based on user preferences and purchase history.

Steps:

1. Collect and preprocess customer data.
2. Use collaborative filtering or AI models to generate recommendations.
3. Integrate the engine into a website or application.

Code Example: Collaborative Filtering Engine *(Refer to Section 22.1.1 for the code.)*

22.5 Practice Problems and Quizzes

22.5.1 Automating E-commerce Workflows with AI

Problem: Write a Python script to predict the top-selling products for the next quarter using historical sales data.

22.5.2 Interactive Quizzes

Question: Which AutoGen application is best suited for inventory management?

1. Product recommendations.
2. Automated reordering.
3. Customer journey enhancement.

Answer: 2. Automated reordering.

22.6 End-of-Chapter Summaries

22.6.1 Key Takeaways

- Personalizing customer experiences drives engagement and sales.
- AutoGen improves inventory tracking and supply chain efficiency.

22.6.2 Quick Reference Guides

Task	Tool/Library	Key Functionality
Product	Scikit-Learn	Suggest products to

Task	Tool/Library	Key Functionality
Recommendations		customers.
Inventory Tracking	Python, Pandas	Monitor stock levels.

22.7 Templates and Tools

22.7.1 Workflow Templates

Template for Product Recommendations:

1. Collect customer interaction data.
2. Apply collaborative filtering or AI models.
3. Display recommendations on product pages.

22.7.2 Scripts and Snippets

Reusable Snippet for Inventory Alerts:

python

```python
def check_inventory(level, reorder_point):
    if level <= reorder_point:
        return "Reorder required"
    return "Stock sufficient"

# Example usage
stock_level = 30
reorder_point = 50
print(check_inventory(stock_level, reorder_point))
```

This chapter provided insights into how AutoGen transforms e-commerce through personalized customer experiences, efficient inventory management, and streamlined supply chain processes. By leveraging the tools, templates, and examples presented, e-commerce businesses can create more engaging and efficient workflows.

Chapter 23: AutoGen in Education

Education is rapidly evolving with the integration of AI and automation, enabling institutions to deliver more efficient, personalized, and impactful learning experiences. AutoGen technologies streamline administrative processes, tailor learning pathways, and enhance student engagement. This chapter explores the key applications of AutoGen in education, backed by case studies, hands-on projects, and actionable resources.

23.1 Automating Administrative Tasks

23.1.1 Streamlining Enrollment and Scheduling Processes

1. Challenges in Enrollment and Scheduling:

- Manual enrollment processes are time-consuming and error-prone.
- Scheduling classes often involves balancing complex variables like teacher availability, room assignments, and student preferences.

2. AutoGen Solutions:

- **Automated Enrollment Systems:** AI-driven workflows process applications, verify documents, and notify applicants.
- **Dynamic Scheduling Algorithms:** Automatically generate optimized class schedules based on constraints.

Code Example: Automating Class Scheduling

python

```
from ortools.sat.python import cp_model
```

```python
# Create model
model = cp_model.CpModel()

# Example: Scheduling 3 classes across 2 rooms
num_classes = 3
num_rooms = 2

# Variables: Class-room assignments
assignments = []
for c in range(num_classes):
    assignments.append([model.NewBoolVar(f"class_{c}_room_{r}") for r in range(num_rooms)])

# Constraints: Each class is assigned to exactly one room
for c in range(num_classes):
    model.Add(sum(assignments[c]) == 1)

# Solve and print schedule
solver = cp_model.CpSolver()
status = solver.Solve(model)
if status == cp_model.OPTIMAL:
    for c in range(num_classes):
        for r in range(num_rooms):
            if solver.Value(assignments[c][r]):
                print(f"Class {c} assigned to Room {r}")
```

23.1.2 Enhancing Communication with Automated Systems

1. Importance of Automated Communication:

- Keeps students, parents, and staff informed about schedules, grades, and events.
- Reduces the administrative burden of handling repetitive inquiries.

2. Applications of AutoGen:

- **Email Notifications:** Automate reminders for deadlines, events, and announcements.
- **Chatbots for FAQs:** Handle common questions, such as admission criteria or exam schedules.

Code Example: Email Notification System

python

```python
import smtplib
from email.mime.text import MIMEText

# Function to send automated emails
def send_email(to_address, subject, message):
    smtp_server = "smtp.example.com"
    sender_email = "admin@example.com"
    password = "yourpassword"

    msg = MIMEText(message)
    msg["Subject"] = subject
    msg["From"] = sender_email
    msg["To"] = to_address

    with smtplib.SMTP(smtp_server, 587) as server:
        server.starttls()
        server.login(sender_email, password)
        server.sendmail(sender_email, to_address, msg.as_string())

# Example usage
send_email("student@example.com", "Exam Reminder", "Your exam is scheduled for Monday at 10 AM.")
```

23.2 Personalized Learning Pathways

23.2.1 Tailoring Educational Content to Individual Needs

1. Importance of Personalization:

- Every student learns at a different pace and has unique needs.
- Personalized learning enhances engagement and retention.

2. AutoGen Applications:

- **Adaptive Learning Platforms:** Use AI to assess student performance and recommend resources.
- **Dynamic Content Delivery:** Tailor quizzes, lessons, and exercises to match a student's progress.

Code Example: Adaptive Learning Algorithm

python

```python
def recommend_next_topic(student_performance):
    topics = ["Basics", "Intermediate", "Advanced"]
    if student_performance < 50:
        return topics[0]  # Basics
    elif student_performance < 80:
        return topics[1]  # Intermediate
    else:
        return topics[2]  # Advanced

# Example
performance = 65
print(f"Recommended Topic: {recommend_next_topic(performance)}")
```

23.2.2 Automating Assessment and Feedback Mechanisms

1. Benefits of Automated Assessments:

- Save time for educators by grading quizzes and assignments automatically.
- Provide immediate feedback to students for continuous improvement.

2. Applications of AI:

- **Essay Grading:** Use NLP to evaluate written responses.
- **Automated Feedback Systems:** Highlight areas of strength and weakness.

Code Example: Grading Multiple-Choice Questions

python

```
def grade_quiz(answers, correct_answers):
    score = sum(1 for a, c in zip(answers, correct_answers) if a == c)
    total = len(correct_answers)
    return f"Score: {score}/{total}"

# Example usage
student_answers = ["A", "B", "C", "D"]
correct_answers = ["A", "B", "C", "A"]
print(grade_quiz(student_answers, correct_answers))
```

23.3 Case Studies

23.3.1 Implementing AutoGen for Virtual Classrooms

Scenario: An online learning platform integrated AutoGen to automate attendance tracking, distribute study materials, and manage class recordings.

Outcome:

- Reduced administrative workload by 50%.
- Improved student satisfaction through efficient resource distribution.

23.3.2 Enhancing Student Engagement with AI Tutors

Scenario: A university deployed AI tutors to provide one-on-one learning support for students in introductory programming courses.

Outcome:

- Increased student engagement by 35%.
- Reduced dropout rates by 20%.

23.4 Hands-On Project

23.4.1 Building an AI-Powered Personalized Learning Platform

Objective: Develop a platform that assesses a student's performance and dynamically generates personalized learning pathways.

Steps:

1. Build a database of topics and exercises.
2. Implement an adaptive algorithm to suggest the next topic.
3. Provide progress tracking and automated feedback.

Code Example: Progress Tracker

python

```python
class ProgressTracker:
    def __init__(self):
        self.progress = {}

    def update_progress(self, student, topic, score):
        if student not in self.progress:
            self.progress[student] = {}
        self.progress[student][topic] = score

    def get_progress(self, student):
        return self.progress.get(student, "No progress found")

# Example usage
tracker = ProgressTracker()
tracker.update_progress("Alice", "Basics", 85)
print(tracker.get_progress("Alice"))
```

23.5 Practice Problems and Quizzes

23.5.1 Applying AutoGen in Educational Settings

Problem: Design a chatbot that answers frequently asked questions about course enrollment.

23.5.2 Interactive Quizzes

Question: Which AutoGen application is best suited for automating feedback mechanisms?

1. Dynamic content delivery.
2. Adaptive assessments.
3. Personalized notifications.

Answer: 2. Adaptive assessments.

23.6 End-of-Chapter Summaries

23.6.1 Key Takeaways

- AutoGen simplifies administrative tasks, enabling educators to focus on teaching.
- Personalized learning pathways enhance student engagement and outcomes.

23.6.2 Quick Reference Guides

Task	Tool/Library	Key Functionality
Automated Scheduling	OR-Tools	Optimize class schedules.
Adaptive Learning	Custom Python Algorithms	Tailor content to student needs.

23.7 Templates and Tools

23.7.1 Workflow Templates

Template for Adaptive Learning:

1. Assess student performance.
2. Recommend resources based on scores.
3. Provide real-time feedback.

23.7.2 Scripts and Snippets

Reusable Snippet for Feedback Generation:

python

```python
def generate_feedback(score):
    if score > 80:
        return "Excellent work! Keep it up."
    elif score > 50:
        return "Good effort. Focus on improving weaker areas."
    else:
        return "Needs improvement. Review the basics."

# Example
print(generate_feedback(75))
```

This chapter showcased how AutoGen transforms education by automating administrative tasks, personalizing learning pathways, and enhancing student engagement. With practical examples, tools, and templates, educators can create more efficient and impactful educational experiences.

Chapter 24: AutoGen in Marketing and Advertising

Marketing and advertising have undergone a significant transformation with the advent of automation and AI. AutoGen enables businesses to streamline campaign management, personalize customer interactions, and generate high-quality content at scale. This chapter explores how AutoGen is reshaping marketing and advertising through advanced automation techniques, real-world case studies, and hands-on projects.

24.1 Automating Campaign Management

24.1.1 Streamlining Ad Creation and Distribution

1. Challenges in Ad Management:

- Creating ads manually for multiple platforms is time-intensive.
- Ensuring consistency across campaigns can be difficult.
- Managing distribution and scheduling requires meticulous planning.

2. AutoGen Solutions:

- **Automated Ad Generation:** Create ads tailored to specific audiences using AI-driven templates.
- **Multi-Platform Distribution:** Automate scheduling and distribution across platforms like Google Ads, Facebook, and Instagram.

Code Example: Automating Ad Creation

python

```python
def generate_ad(template, product_name, audience):
    return template.format(product=product_name, audience=audience)

# Example usage
template = "Introducing {product}, perfect for {audience}. Click to learn more!"
ad = generate_ad(template, "SmartWatch X", "fitness enthusiasts")
print(ad)
```

24.1.2 Enhancing Targeting and Personalization with AI

1. Benefits of AI-Driven Targeting:

- Identifies high-value customer segments through data analysis.
- Personalizes messages based on user preferences and behavior.

2. Techniques:

- **Behavioral Analysis:** Track user interactions to create targeted campaigns.
- **Predictive Analytics:** Forecast customer needs based on past data.

Code Example: Customer Segmentation

python

```python
import pandas as pd
from sklearn.cluster import KMeans

# Sample customer data
data = {
    "Age": [25, 34, 45, 23, 31],
    "SpendingScore": [77, 60, 88, 45, 59]
}
```

```
df = pd.DataFrame(data)

# Apply KMeans clustering
kmeans = KMeans(n_clusters=2)
df["Segment"] = kmeans.fit_predict(df)

print(df)
```

24.2 Content Generation for Marketing

24.2.1 Automating Blog Posts, Social Media, and Email Campaigns

1. AI Tools for Content Creation:

- **Blog Posts:** Generate long-form articles using GPT-based models.
- **Social Media:** Craft catchy captions and hashtags.
- **Email Campaigns:** Personalize subject lines and email content.

2. Benefits:

- Reduces the time spent on repetitive content creation.
- Ensures consistency and quality across platforms.

Code Example: Automated Email Campaign

python

```
def generate_email(subject_template, body_template, customer_name, product):
    subject = subject_template.format(customer=customer_name)
    body = body_template.format(customer=customer_name, product=product)
    return {"subject": subject, "body": body}
```

```
# Example templates
subject_template = "Hi {customer}, your perfect product is here!"
body_template = "Dear {customer}, check out our new {product}. Available now!"

# Generate email
email = generate_email(subject_template, body_template, "Alice", "SmartWatch X")
print(email)
```

24.2.2 Enhancing Creativity with AI-Driven Content Tools

1. Creative Applications of AI:

- Generate visual assets like banners or logos using tools like DALL-E or Canva AI.
- Create engaging video ads with AI-driven video editing tools.

2. Examples of Tools:

- **Text-Based Content:** Jasper, Writesonic.
- **Visual Content:** MidJourney, Adobe Firefly.

24.3 Case Studies

24.3.1 Implementing AutoGen for Automated Social Media Management

Scenario: A clothing retailer implemented AutoGen to automate social media posting, including caption creation and hashtag recommendations.

Outcome:

- Increased follower engagement by 25%.
- Reduced the workload of their social media team by 50%.

24.3.2 Enhancing Marketing ROI with AI-Driven Campaigns

Scenario: A SaaS company used AutoGen to identify high-value customers and personalize marketing campaigns.

Outcome:

- Achieved a 30% increase in conversion rates.
- Reduced customer acquisition costs by 20%.

24.4 Hands-On Project

24.4.1 Developing an AI-Powered Marketing Campaign Manager

Objective: Build a tool that automates campaign creation, scheduling, and performance monitoring.

Steps:

1. Collect customer data for segmentation.
2. Generate campaign content using predefined templates.
3. Integrate with APIs for scheduling and analytics.

Code Example: Campaign Scheduler

python

```python
import schedule
import time

# Function to post campaign
def post_campaign():
    print("Campaign posted to social media!")
```

```
# Schedule campaign
schedule.every().monday.at("10:00").do(post_campaign)

# Keep script running
while True:
    schedule.run_pending()
    time.sleep(1)
```

24.5 Practice Problems and Quizzes

24.5.1 Leveraging AutoGen for Marketing Automation

Problem: Write a Python script to generate dynamic product descriptions for an e-commerce website.

24.5.2 Interactive Quizzes

Question: Which AI tool is best suited for personalized email campaigns?

1. Tableau.
2. GPT-based models.
3. OR-Tools.

Answer: 2. GPT-based models.

24.6 End-of-Chapter Summaries

24.6.1 Key Takeaways

- AutoGen automates marketing tasks such as ad creation, campaign management, and content generation.

- AI enhances personalization, improving customer engagement and ROI.

24.6.2 Quick Reference Guides

Task	Tool/Library	Key Functionality
Campaign Automation	Python, Schedule	Automate ad scheduling.
Customer Segmentation	Scikit-Learn	Analyze customer data.

24.7 Templates and Tools

24.7.1 Workflow Templates

Template for Email Campaigns:

1. Collect customer data.
2. Generate email content using templates.
3. Schedule and monitor email performance.

24.7.2 Scripts and Snippets

Reusable Snippet for Ad Personalization:

python

```python
def personalize_ad(ad_template, product, audience):
    return ad_template.format(product=product, audience=audience)

# Example usage
template = "Discover {product} - perfect for {audience}!"
ad = personalize_ad(template, "SmartWatch X", "tech enthusiasts")
print(ad)
```

AutoGen is revolutionizing marketing and advertising by automating repetitive tasks, personalizing customer interactions, and enhancing creativity. This chapter equips marketers with tools, templates, and real-world examples to streamline their campaigns and achieve greater impact with minimal effort.

Chapter 25: AutoGen in Manufacturing

Manufacturing is at the forefront of innovation through automation and AI. AutoGen technologies enable manufacturers to streamline production, optimize supply chains, enhance quality control, and predict maintenance needs. This chapter explores how AutoGen is revolutionizing manufacturing, with detailed case studies, hands-on projects, and actionable tools to implement these technologies effectively.

25.1 Automating Production Processes

25.1.1 Streamlining Assembly Line Operations

1. Challenges in Assembly Lines:

- Bottlenecks in production due to manual workflows.
- Errors introduced by human intervention in repetitive tasks.
- Difficulty in tracking performance metrics across multiple lines.

2. AutoGen Solutions:

- **AI-Powered Robotics:** Use robotic systems to automate repetitive tasks like assembling, welding, or packaging.
- **Process Monitoring:** Employ sensors and AI to monitor assembly line performance in real time.

Code Example: Monitoring Assembly Line Efficiency

python

```
import random
```

```python
# Simulate assembly line efficiency
def monitor_efficiency():
    efficiency = random.uniform(80, 100)  # Efficiency in percentage
    if efficiency < 90:
        return f"Warning: Efficiency dropped to {efficiency:.2f}%"
    return f"Efficiency is at {efficiency:.2f}%"

# Monitor efficiency
print(monitor_efficiency())
```

25.1.2 Enhancing Quality Control with AI

1. Benefits of AI in Quality Control:

- Detect defects more accurately than manual inspection.
- Reduce wastage by identifying errors early in the process.

2. Techniques for Automated Quality Control:

- **Computer Vision:** Use AI to analyze images of products for defects.
- **Anomaly Detection Models:** Flag outliers in production metrics that indicate quality issues.

Code Example: Detecting Defects with Computer Vision

python

```python
from tensorflow.keras.models import load_model
from tensorflow.keras.preprocessing.image import load_img, img_to_array

# Load pre-trained model
model = load_model("quality_control_model.h5")

# Analyze product image
```

```python
image = load_img("product_sample.jpg", target_size=(224, 224))
image_array = img_to_array(image).reshape(1, 224, 224, 3)
prediction = model.predict(image_array)
if prediction[0] > 0.5:
    print("Defective product detected")
else:
    print("Product passed quality control")
```

25.2 Predictive Maintenance and Supply Chain Optimization

25.2.1 Automating Equipment Monitoring and Maintenance Scheduling

1. Importance of Predictive Maintenance:

- Prevents costly downtime by predicting failures before they occur.
- Extends the lifespan of machinery through timely interventions.

2. AutoGen Techniques:

- **IoT Sensors:** Collect real-time data from machines.
- **AI Models:** Predict maintenance needs based on sensor data.

Code Example: Predicting Equipment Failure

python

```python
import numpy as np
from sklearn.linear_model import LogisticRegression

# Simulated sensor data
```

```python
sensor_readings = np.array([[70, 1], [85, 0], [95, 1], [60, 0], [90, 1]])  # [Temp, Failure]
X, y = sensor_readings[:, 0].reshape(-1, 1), sensor_readings[:, 1]

# Train model
model = LogisticRegression()
model.fit(X, y)

# Predict maintenance need
temp = 80  # Current temperature
prediction = model.predict([[temp]])
print("Maintenance required" if prediction[0] == 1 else "No maintenance needed")
```

25.2.2 Optimizing Supply Chain Logistics with AI Models

1. Challenges in Supply Chain Management:

- Inefficiencies in transportation and storage.
- Difficulty in demand forecasting.

2. AI-Powered Solutions:

- **Demand Forecasting:** Use AI models to predict future demand and adjust inventory levels.
- **Route Optimization:** Minimize transportation costs by optimizing delivery routes.

Code Example: Demand Forecasting with Time Series Analysis

python

```python
from statsmodels.tsa.arima_model import ARIMA
import numpy as np

# Simulated demand data
```

```
demand_data = np.array([100, 120, 130, 125, 140])

# Fit ARIMA model
model = ARIMA(demand_data, order=(1, 1, 1))
model_fit = model.fit(disp=0)

# Forecast future demand
forecast = model_fit.forecast(steps=3)[0]
print("Forecasted demand:", forecast)
```

25.3 Case Studies

25.3.1 Implementing AutoGen for Smart Factories

Scenario: A large-scale manufacturer implemented AutoGen to automate production workflows and monitor equipment performance in real time.

Outcome:

- Reduced downtime by 30% through predictive maintenance.
- Improved overall equipment effectiveness (OEE) by 25%.

25.3.2 Enhancing Manufacturing Efficiency with Predictive Maintenance

Scenario: An automotive parts manufacturer deployed IoT sensors and AutoGen workflows to monitor the health of assembly line machines.

Outcome:

- Prevented catastrophic failures by predicting and addressing issues in advance.
- Saved $1 million annually in repair and downtime costs.

25.4 Hands-On Project

25.4.1 Building an AI-Driven Production Monitoring System

Objective: Create a system that monitors production metrics and alerts operators when anomalies are detected.

Steps:

1. Collect real-time sensor data from production lines.
2. Use AI models to detect anomalies in the data.
3. Generate alerts for potential issues.

Code Example: Anomaly Detection in Production Metrics

python

```python
from sklearn.ensemble import IsolationForest
import numpy as np

# Simulated production data
data = np.array([[100], [102], [98], [95], [300]])  # Last value is an anomaly

# Train Isolation Forest
clf = IsolationForest(contamination=0.1)
clf.fit(data)

# Predict anomalies
predictions = clf.predict(data)
print("Anomalies detected:", data[predictions == -1])
```

25.5 Practice Problems and Quizzes

25.5.1 Applying AutoGen in Manufacturing Workflows

Problem: Write a Python script to calculate the reorder point for raw materials in an assembly line.

25.5.2 Interactive Quizzes

Question: Which technique is best suited for detecting product defects in a manufacturing workflow?

1. Logistic Regression.
2. Computer Vision.
3. ARIMA Model.

Answer: 2. Computer Vision.

25.6 End-of-Chapter Summaries

25.6.1 Key Takeaways

- AutoGen enhances efficiency in manufacturing by automating assembly lines, quality control, and maintenance.
- Predictive maintenance and supply chain optimization reduce costs and improve operational reliability.

25.6.2 Quick Reference Guides

Task	Tool/Library	Key Functionality
Quality Control	TensorFlow	Detect defects in products.
Predictive Maintenance	Scikit-Learn	Predict equipment failures.

25.7 Templates and Tools

25.7.1 Workflow Templates

Template for Predictive Maintenance:

1. Collect real-time data from IoT sensors.
2. Train a machine learning model to predict failures.
3. Automate alerts and maintenance scheduling.

25.7.2 Scripts and Snippets

Reusable Snippet for Supply Chain Optimization:

python

```python
def optimize_route(locations):
    # Simulate route optimization logic
    return sorted(locations)

# Example usage
locations = ["Warehouse A", "Factory B", "Retail Store C"]
optimized_route = optimize_route(locations)
print("Optimized Route:", optimized_route)
```

AutoGen is transforming manufacturing by automating production, enhancing quality control, and optimizing supply chains. This chapter equips manufacturers with actionable insights and tools to implement AI-driven workflows that improve efficiency, reduce costs, and ensure reliability.

Part V: Future Trends and Innovations in AutoGen

Chapter 26: Emerging Trends in AI-Driven Automation

As automation evolves, advancements in AI technologies are shaping the future of workflow automation and business processes. AutoGen remains at the forefront of this evolution, integrating next-generation AI models, improving human-AI collaboration, and driving digital transformation across industries. This chapter explores the latest trends and innovations in AI-driven automation, providing a comprehensive guide to emerging technologies and their applications.

26.1 Advances in Generative AI

26.1.1 Next-Generation LLMs and Their Capabilities

1. Evolution of Large Language Models (LLMs):

- **Scalability:** From GPT-4 to emerging models like GPT-5 and LLaMA 3, newer LLMs are larger, faster, and more capable.

- **Fine-Tuning:** Enhanced customization allows domain-specific applications, such as legal, healthcare, or financial contexts.

- **Contextual Understanding:** Newer models handle longer contexts, enabling deeper and more coherent outputs.

2. Applications:

- Automating report generation and technical documentation.

- Enhancing conversational AI for more natural interactions.

Example Code: Using an LLM API for Report Generation

python

```python
import openai

# Connect to OpenAI API
openai.api_key = "your-api-key"

# Generate a report
prompt = "Generate a detailed summary of emerging trends in AI for a business report."
response = openai.Completion.create(
    engine="text-davinci-004",
    prompt=prompt,
    max_tokens=500
)
print(response.choices[0].text.strip())
```

26.1.2 Innovations in Multi-Modal AI Systems

1. Definition and Capabilities:

- Multi-modal AI systems combine text, image, audio, and video inputs for more comprehensive outputs.
- Models like OpenAI's DALL-E 3 and Google's DeepMind Gemini integrate multiple data types seamlessly.

2. Applications:

- **Content Creation:** Generate both textual and visual marketing materials.
- **Data Analysis:** Combine text-based reports with visual charts.

Example Code: Integrating Text and Image Generation

python

```
# Text and image generation using OpenAI's API
text_prompt = "Create a marketing tagline for a new eco-friendly product."
image_prompt = "Generate an image of eco-friendly packaging with a natural theme."

# Generate text
text_response = openai.Completion.create(
    engine="text-davinci-004",
    prompt=text_prompt,
    max_tokens=50
)
print("Tagline:", text_response.choices[0].text.strip())

# Generate image (using a hypothetical API for visualization)
image_response = openai.Image.create(prompt=image_prompt, n=1, size="512x512")
print("Generated Image URL:", image_response["data"][0]["url"])
```

26.2 AI and Human Collaboration

26.2.1 Enhancing Human-AI Interaction

1. Features of Human-AI Interaction:

- **Natural Interfaces:** Use conversational AI and voice commands for seamless interactions.
- **Feedback Loops:** Systems that learn and adapt based on user feedback.

2. Applications:

- **Virtual Assistants:** Assist in daily tasks like scheduling or drafting emails.
- **Interactive Dashboards:** Provide insights with real-time interaction.

Example Code: Conversational AI Integration

python

```python
def virtual_assistant(user_input):
    response = openai.Completion.create(
        engine="text-davinci-004",
        prompt=f"Assistant: {user_input}",
        max_tokens=100
    )
    return response.choices[0].text.strip()

# Example interaction
print(virtual_assistant("What are the latest trends in AI?"))
```

26.2.2 Synergizing Human Creativity with AI Automation

1. Collaborative Creativity:

- AI augments human creativity by providing suggestions or generating ideas.
- Applications include brainstorming sessions, content ideation, and creative design.

2. Real-World Applications:

- Generating ad campaign ideas collaboratively with teams and AI.
- Using AI tools for preliminary design drafts in architecture or product development.

26.3 The Role of AI in Digital Transformation

26.3.1 Driving Organizational Change with AI

1. Benefits of AI in Transformation:

- Speeds up decision-making by analyzing large datasets.
- Improves operational efficiency through automation.

2. Key Areas:

- **HR:** Automating recruitment processes.
- **Finance:** Enhancing financial forecasting.

Case Example: AI-Driven Digital Transformation

text

A multinational corporation reduced operational costs by 40% by integrating AI into supply chain management, optimizing inventory, and automating logistics planning.

26.3.2 Case Studies on Successful AI Integration

Case Study 1: E-commerce Platform

- **Challenge:** Personalized marketing at scale.
- **Solution:** Deployed AutoGen to analyze customer data and recommend products dynamically.
- **Outcome:** 30% increase in sales conversions.

Case Study 2: Healthcare Provider

- **Challenge:** Reduce patient wait times.
- **Solution:** AI-powered scheduling systems to optimize doctor availability.
- **Outcome:** 50% reduction in average patient wait time.

26.4 Predictive and Prescriptive Analytics

26.4.1 Moving Beyond Descriptive Analytics

1. Predictive Analytics:

- Use historical data to forecast future trends.
- Applications include sales forecasting and risk assessment.

2. Prescriptive Analytics:

- Recommends actions based on predictions.
- Common in supply chain optimization and financial planning.

Code Example: Predictive Sales Analysis

python

```python
from sklearn.linear_model import LinearRegression
import numpy as np

# Simulated data
X = np.array([1, 2, 3, 4, 5]).reshape(-1, 1)  # Months
y = np.array([1000, 1200, 1300, 1500, 1700])  # Sales

# Train model
model = LinearRegression()
model.fit(X, y)

# Predict future sales
future_months = np.array([6, 7, 8]).reshape(-1, 1)
predictions = model.predict(future_months)
print("Predicted Sales:", predictions)
```

26.4.2 Automating Decision-Making Processes with AI

1. **Decision Trees and Neural Networks:**
   - Automate complex decision-making by analyzing multiple variables.

2. **Applications:**
   - **Customer Support:** AI triages support tickets.
   - **Manufacturing:** Automates production scheduling.

26.5 Hands-On Project

26.5.1 Exploring Cutting-Edge AI Technologies in Workflow Automation

Objective: Build a workflow automation tool that integrates predictive analytics, multi-modal AI, and human-AI collaboration.

Steps:

1. Collect and preprocess data.
2. Implement AI for predictions and recommendations.
3. Build an interactive dashboard for human feedback.

Code Example: Workflow Integration

python

```
import dash
from dash import dcc, html

app = dash.Dash(__name__)

app.layout = html.Div([
    html.H1("AI-Driven Workflow Dashboard"),
    dcc.Input(id="user_input", type="text", placeholder="Enter command"),
```

```
    html.Button("Submit", id="submit_btn"),
    html.Div(id="output")
])

if __name__ == '__main__':
    app.run_server(debug=True)
```

26.6 Practice Problems and Quizzes

26.6.1 Understanding Emerging Trends in AutoGen

Problem: Explain the role of multi-modal AI in enhancing workflow automation.

26.6.2 Interactive Quizzes

Question: Which feature is unique to multi-modal AI systems?

1. Contextual text generation.
2. Integrating text and images.
3. Predictive analytics.

Answer: 2. Integrating text and images.

26.7 End-of-Chapter Summaries

26.7.1 Key Takeaways

- Advances in AI, particularly in multi-modal systems and LLMs, are transforming automation.
- Predictive and prescriptive analytics enhance decision-making efficiency.

26.7.2 Quick Reference Guides

Task	Tool/Library	Key Functionality
Predictive Analytics	Scikit-Learn	Forecast trends.
Multi-Modal AI	OpenAI, TensorFlow	Integrate text, images, and more.

26.8 Templates and Tools

26.8.1 Workflow Templates

Template for Predictive Analytics:

1. Collect historical data.
2. Train a machine learning model.
3. Automate predictions and actions.

26.8.2 Scripts and Snippets

Reusable Snippet for Multi-Modal Integration:

python

```
def generate_multi_modal_content(text_prompt, image_prompt):
    text = openai.Completion.create(engine="text-davinci-004", prompt=text_prompt)
    image = openai.Image.create(prompt=image_prompt)
    return text.choices[0].text.strip(), image["data"][0]["url"]

text, image_url = generate_multi_modal_content("Write a tagline", "Create an eco-friendly product image")
print("Text:", text)
```

```
print("Image URL:", image_url)
```

This chapter outlined the emerging trends in AI-driven automation, highlighting advancements in LLMs, multi-modal AI, predictive analytics, and human-AI collaboration. These innovations pave the way for more intelligent, adaptive, and impactful automation solutions.

Chapter 27: The Future of AutoGen

The rapid evolution of AI and automation heralds a transformative future for industries and societies. As AutoGen technologies continue to advance, ensuring ethical practices, preparing for emerging innovations, and adopting strategic planning are critical for success. This chapter examines the future of AutoGen, covering governance, ethical considerations, technological advancements, and the skills needed for an AI-driven world. Practical tools, templates, and hands-on projects provide actionable insights for navigating the road ahead.

27.1 AI Governance and Policy

27.1.1 Developing Frameworks for Responsible AI

1. Importance of AI Governance:

- Ensures AI systems are aligned with societal values and legal requirements.
- Protects against risks such as bias, misuse, and data breaches.

2. Key Components of AI Governance Frameworks:

- **Accountability:** Establish roles and responsibilities for AI oversight.
- **Transparency:** Ensure AI models and decisions are explainable.
- **Auditing:** Conduct regular audits to assess compliance with ethical standards.

Example Framework:

Aspect	Key Actions
Accountability	Define AI governance roles.
Transparency	Publish model decision-making processes.
Risk Management	Identify and mitigate potential risks.

27.1.2 Navigating Regulatory Landscapes

1. Global AI Regulations:

- **EU:** General Data Protection Regulation (GDPR) and AI Act.
- **US:** AI Bill of Rights and sector-specific regulations.
- **China:** Guidelines on algorithm transparency and fairness.

2. Strategies for Compliance:

- **Proactive Audits:** Identify regulatory gaps in AI workflows.
- **Data Governance:** Ensure data handling meets privacy standards.

Code Example: Anonymizing Sensitive Data

python

```
import pandas as pd

# Sample data
data = pd.DataFrame({
    "Name": ["Alice", "Bob", "Charlie"],
    "SSN": ["123-45-6789", "987-65-4321", "456-78-9123"]
})

# Anonymize SSNs
```

```
data["SSN"] = data["SSN"].apply(lambda x: "XXX-XX-" + x.split("-")[2])
print(data)
```

27.2 Ethical AI and Social Impact

27.2.1 Balancing Automation with Human Employment

1. The Challenge:

- Automation risks displacing workers, particularly in repetitive, low-skill roles.

2. Solutions:

- **Reskilling Programs:** Train employees for roles in managing and augmenting AI systems.
- **Augmented Workflows:** Combine human creativity with AI efficiency.

Case Example: Augmented Manufacturing

text

A manufacturing company implemented AI for quality control while retraining its workforce to manage automated systems. This approach reduced errors and retained employment levels.

27.2.2 Ensuring Inclusive and Fair AI Practices

1. Risks of Exclusion:

- Bias in training data can marginalize specific groups.
- AI systems may inadvertently reinforce existing inequalities.

2. Best Practices:

- **Diverse Data Sets:** Use representative data for model training.

- **Bias Auditing:** Regularly evaluate models for fairness.

Code Example: Bias Detection in a Dataset

python

```
import pandas as pd

# Sample dataset
data = pd.DataFrame({
    "Gender": ["Male", "Female", "Male", "Female", "Male"],
    "Salary": [50000, 52000, 48000, 50000, 49000]
})

# Check for salary disparity by gender
gender_groups = data.groupby("Gender")["Salary"].mean()
print(gender_groups)
```

27.3 Innovations in AutoGen Technology

27.3.1 Integrating AI with Quantum Computing

1. Potential of Quantum-AI Integration:

- **Speed:** Quantum computing can exponentially accelerate complex computations.
- **Optimization:** Solves large-scale optimization problems more effectively.

2. Applications:

- Supply chain optimization and large-scale simulations.
- Faster training of AI models.

27.3.2 Future-Proofing AutoGen Systems

1. **Importance of Adaptability:**
   - Technology evolves rapidly; systems must adapt to remain relevant.

2. **Strategies:**
   - **Modular Architectures:** Design systems that can integrate new components seamlessly.
   - **Continuous Learning:** Use AI that updates based on new data.

Code Example: Modular Workflow

```python
def process_data(module, data):
    return module(data)

# Example modules
def clean_data(data):
    return data.strip()

def analyze_data(data):
    return f"Analysis of {data}"

# Use case
data = " Raw Input "
processed_data = process_data(clean_data, data)
analysis = process_data(analyze_data, processed_data)
print(analysis)
```

27.4 Preparing for the AI-Driven Future

27.4.1 Skills and Competencies for the Next Generation

1. **Key Skills:**
    - **Data Literacy:** Understanding AI inputs, outputs, and implications.
    - **Ethics:** Navigating the societal and ethical impacts of AI.
    - **Collaboration:** Working effectively alongside AI systems.

27.4.2 Strategic Planning for Long-Term AI Integration

1. **Aligning AI with Organizational Goals:**
    - Develop a roadmap for AI adoption that includes stakeholder input.
    - Regularly assess progress and adjust strategies.

2. **Metrics for Success:**
    - ROI from AI projects.
    - Employee and customer satisfaction.

27.5 Hands-On Project

27.5.1 Designing a Future-Ready AutoGen Strategy for an Organization

Objective: Create a strategic roadmap for integrating AutoGen technologies into a business.

Steps:
1. Identify business needs.
2. Map AutoGen capabilities to specific goals.
3. Develop a phased implementation plan.

27.6 Practice Problems and Quizzes

27.6.1 Anticipating and Preparing for Future Developments

Problem: Design a strategy for adopting AI governance frameworks in an organization.

27.6.2 Interactive Quizzes

Question: What is a key advantage of integrating AI with quantum computing?

1. Increased interpretability.
2. Faster computation speeds.
3. Reduced training data requirements.

Answer: 2. Faster computation speeds.

27.7 End-of-Chapter Summaries

27.7.1 Key Takeaways

- Governance frameworks ensure ethical and responsible AI use.
- Emerging technologies like quantum computing will redefine AutoGen's capabilities.

27.7.2 Quick Reference Guides

Task	Tool/Library	Key Functionality
Bias Detection	Pandas	Analyze datasets for fairness.
Data Anonymization	Python	Protect sensitive information.

27.8 Templates and Tools

27.8.1 Workflow Templates

Template for Ethical AI Integration:

1. Conduct a fairness audit.
2. Ensure diverse data representation.
3. Implement explainability measures.

27.8.2 Scripts and Snippets

Reusable Snippet for Compliance Reporting:

python

```python
def generate_compliance_report(data):
    # Example compliance checks
    issues = []
    if "SSN" in data.columns:
        issues.append("Sensitive data detected: SSN")
    return issues or "No compliance issues detected"

# Example usage
data = pd.DataFrame({"SSN": ["123-45-6789"]})
print(generate_compliance_report(data))
```

The future of AutoGen hinges on ethical practices, adaptability, and strategic planning. By embracing innovations like quantum computing and fostering collaboration between AI and humans, organizations can unlock unprecedented potential while ensuring responsible use.

Part VI: Community, Resources, and Supplementary Materials

Chapter 28: Building and Leveraging the AutoGen Community

The AutoGen ecosystem thrives on collaboration, shared knowledge, and active participation. Building and leveraging this community allows individuals and organizations to accelerate learning, solve complex problems, and contribute to the broader field of AI-driven automation. This chapter provides an in-depth guide to engaging with the AutoGen community, fostering collaborations, and contributing meaningfully to the ecosystem.

28.1 Engaging with the AutoGen Ecosystem

28.1.1 Joining Forums and Online Communities

1. Importance of Online Communities:

- Access to diverse perspectives and solutions.
- Networking opportunities with industry professionals and enthusiasts.
- Staying updated on the latest trends and tools in AutoGen.

2. Recommended Platforms:

- **Reddit Communities:** Subreddits like r/MachineLearning or r/AutoGen.
- **Stack Overflow:** For technical questions and code troubleshooting.
- **GitHub:** Explore repositories and contribute to open-source AutoGen projects.

Example: Searching GitHub for AutoGen Projects

bash

```
# Using the GitHub search bar:
search query: "AutoGen workflows language:Python"
```

3. Tips for Engagement:

- Participate in discussions by asking insightful questions.
- Share your experiences, challenges, and solutions.
- Respect community guidelines to foster a collaborative environment.

28.1.2 Participating in Open-Source Projects

1. Benefits of Contributing:

- Enhance your skills by working on real-world projects.
- Gain recognition in the community.
- Build a portfolio of contributions to showcase your expertise.

2. Steps to Contribute:

- Identify repositories needing help (search for labels like help-wanted or good-first-issue on GitHub).
- Fork the repository and start working on issues.
- Submit pull requests with clear descriptions of changes.

Code Example: Setting Up a GitHub Repository for an AutoGen Project

bash

```
# Initialize a GitHub repository
git init AutoGen-Project
git add .
git commit -m "Initial commit"
```

git remote add origin https://github.com/yourusername/AutoGen-Project.git

git push -u origin main

28.2 Collaborating with Peers and Experts

28.2.1 Networking Strategies

1. Attend Industry Events:

- Conferences such as **NeurIPS**, **ICML**, or **AI Expo**.
- Virtual meetups and webinars specific to AutoGen technologies.

2. Utilize Social Media:

- Join LinkedIn groups focusing on AI and automation.
- Follow thought leaders and actively engage with their content.

28.2.2 Leveraging Community Knowledge for Problem-Solving

1. Peer Collaboration:

- Share unresolved issues on forums and solicit feedback.
- Collaborate with community members on joint projects.

2. Knowledge Repositories:

- Use shared documents, open-source codebases, and tutorials for self-learning.
- Regularly contribute your findings to benefit others.

\

28.3 Contributing to the AutoGen Field

28.3.1 Sharing Your Projects and Insights

1. Platforms for Sharing:

- Blog on Medium or Dev.to about your projects.
- Publish code repositories on GitHub.

2. Showcase Formats:

- Write tutorials with clear instructions and examples.
- Include screenshots or videos demonstrating your AutoGen workflows.

28.3.2 Writing and Presenting in Conferences

1. Preparing a Conference Paper:

- Highlight novel applications or insights.
- Include data, visuals, and case studies to support your findings.

2. Presentation Tips:

- Use slides with minimal text and clear visuals.
- Practice your talk and anticipate audience questions.

28.4 Case Studies

28.4.1 Successful Community-Driven AutoGen Projects

Example 1: Workflow Automation Repository

- A GitHub repository developed by a global community provided reusable scripts for automating diverse tasks, from email marketing to data cleaning.

Example 2: Open-Source AutoGen Framework

- A team of contributors collaborated to create a modular AutoGen framework, which has since been adopted by startups and enterprises.

28.4.2 Leveraging Community Support for Project Success

Example: Troubleshooting AI Pipelines

- A machine learning engineer resolved deployment challenges by seeking advice from community forums, resulting in a successful product launch.

28.5 Hands-On Project

28.5.1 Initiating and Managing a Community-Based AutoGen Project

Objective: Create an open-source project that invites community collaboration on a unique AutoGen application.

Steps:

1. Define the project scope (e.g., an AutoGen tool for educational content).
2. Set up a GitHub repository with clear contribution guidelines.
3. Promote the project in relevant forums and social media channels.

Code Example: CONTRIBUTING.md File for a GitHub Project

markdown

Contributing to AutoGen Tool

How to Contribute
1. Fork the repository.
2. Clone your fork to your local machine.
3. Create a new branch for your feature or bug fix.
4. Commit your changes with clear messages.
5. Submit a pull request for review.

Guidelines
- Ensure your code follows the project's style guide.
- Include tests for new features.
- Respect the code of conduct.

28.6 Practice Problems and Quizzes

28.6.1 Building and Sustaining a Community around AutoGen

Problem: Draft a strategy to engage contributors for an open-source AutoGen project.

28.6.2 Interactive Quizzes

Question: Which of the following is NOT a recommended platform for engaging with the AutoGen community?

1. GitHub.
2. Reddit.
3. Netflix.

Answer: 3. Netflix.

28.7 End-of-Chapter Summaries

28.7.1 Key Takeaways

- Engaging with the AutoGen community accelerates learning and fosters collaboration.
- Sharing knowledge and contributing to open-source projects are essential for personal and professional growth.

28.7.2 Quick Reference Guides

Task	Platform/Tool	Key Functionality
Joining Communities	Reddit, GitHub	Engage in discussions.
Sharing Projects	Medium, GitHub	Publish tutorials and repositories.

28.8 Templates and Tools

28.8.1 Workflow Templates

Template for Open-Source Project Collaboration:

1. Define project goals and scope.
2. Set up a repository with clear documentation.
3. Invite contributions through forums and social media.

28.8.2 Scripts and Snippets

Reusable Snippet for Community Contribution Tracking:

python

```
import pandas as pd

# Sample contributor data
```

```python
contributors = pd.DataFrame({
    "Name": ["Alice", "Bob", "Charlie"],
    "Contributions": [10, 5, 8]
})

# Sort by contributions
top_contributors = contributors.sort_values("Contributions", ascending=False)
print(top_contributors)
```

The AutoGen community is a vital resource for learning, collaboration, and innovation. By engaging actively, contributing meaningfully, and leveraging the collective knowledge of the community, individuals and organizations can maximize their impact in the field of automation.

Chapter 29: Troubleshooting and Optimization Techniques

Effective troubleshooting and optimization are critical for maintaining robust and efficient AutoGen workflows. This chapter explores common issues, practical optimization strategies, and advanced debugging techniques to ensure your AutoGen systems deliver peak performance. Through case studies, hands-on projects, and actionable tools, readers will gain a comprehensive understanding of how to diagnose problems and optimize workflows.

29.1 Common Issues in AutoGen Workflows

29.1.1 Identifying and Diagnosing Problems

1. Symptoms of Common Issues:

- **Performance Lag:** Delays in executing workflows.
- **Workflow Errors:** Unhandled exceptions or incomplete outputs.
- **Data Inconsistencies:** Incorrect or missing data in the pipeline.

2. Diagnosis Techniques:

- **Error Logs:** Review logs to pinpoint issues.
- **Debugging Tools:** Use IDE debugging features to step through code.
- **Profiling:** Identify bottlenecks using performance profiling tools.

Example: Identifying Bottlenecks in Code

python

```python
import time

def process_data():
    start_time = time.time()
    # Simulated processing
    time.sleep(2)
    print("Processing completed in:", time.time() - start_time, "seconds")

process_data()
```

29.1.2 Best Practices for Troubleshooting

1. Proactive Troubleshooting:

- Use version control to track changes.
- Implement automated testing to catch issues early.

2. Structured Debugging Steps:

- **Step 1:** Replicate the problem in a controlled environment.
- **Step 2:** Isolate components to find the root cause.
- **Step 3:** Implement and test fixes systematically.

Checklist for Troubleshooting:

Step	Action
Log Analysis	Review error messages and logs.
Configuration Check	Verify setup and dependencies.
Unit Testing	Test individual components.

29.2 Optimization Strategies

29.2.1 Enhancing Performance and Efficiency

1. Techniques for Performance Improvement:

- **Asynchronous Processing:** Run tasks concurrently to save time.
- **Caching:** Store frequently accessed data to reduce computation.
- **Code Optimization:** Refactor code to eliminate inefficiencies.

Example: Asynchronous Workflow Execution

python

```python
import asyncio

async def task(name, duration):
    await asyncio.sleep(duration)
    print(f"Task {name} completed in {duration} seconds")

async def main():
    await asyncio.gather(
        task("A", 2),
        task("B", 3),
        task("C", 1)
    )

asyncio.run(main())
```

29.2.2 Cost Optimization Techniques

1. Reducing Cloud Expenses:

- Use serverless architectures to scale on-demand.
- Optimize resource allocation by monitoring usage patterns.

2. Automation Savings:

- Implement AutoGen solutions to reduce manual interventions and save time.

29.3 Advanced Debugging Techniques

29.3.1 Utilizing Logs and Monitoring Tools

1. Setting Up Logging:

- Enable structured logging for actionable insights.

Code Example: Configuring Logging

python

```
import logging

logging.basicConfig(level=logging.INFO, format='%(asctime)s - %(levelname)s - %(message)s')
logging.info("Workflow started")
try:
    # Simulated task
    raise ValueError("An error occurred")
except Exception as e:
    logging.error(f"Error: {e}")
```

2. Tools for Monitoring:

- **Prometheus** and **Grafana**: For real-time metrics.
- **ELK Stack**: Centralized log management and analysis.

29.3.2 Implementing Automated Debugging Solutions

1. AI-Powered Debugging:

- Use AI models to analyze logs and suggest fixes.

2. Workflow Validation:

- Implement automated testing pipelines to catch issues before deployment.

Example: Automated Testing Framework

python

```
import unittest

def add_numbers(a, b):
    return a + b

class TestMathFunctions(unittest.TestCase):
    def test_add_numbers(self):
        self.assertEqual(add_numbers(2, 3), 5)
        self.assertEqual(add_numbers(-1, 1), 0)

if __name__ == "__main__":
    unittest.main()
```

29.4 Case Studies

29.4.1 Resolving Common Challenges in AutoGen Implementations

Scenario: A retail company faced slow execution times in its inventory automation workflow. After profiling, they identified inefficient database queries as the root cause.

Solution:

- Refactored queries using indexing.
- Implemented caching for frequently accessed data.

Outcome:

- Execution time improved by 40%.

29.4.2 Optimizing Workflows for Peak Performance

Scenario: A logistics firm struggled with high cloud costs due to overprovisioned resources.

Solution:

- Switched to serverless architecture.
- Used predictive scaling based on historical data.

Outcome:

- Achieved a 25% reduction in cloud expenses.

29.5 Hands-On Project

29.5.1 Troubleshooting and Optimizing an Existing AutoGen Workflow

Objective: Diagnose and optimize a workflow experiencing delays and errors.

Steps:

1. Analyze logs to identify errors.
2. Use a profiler to detect bottlenecks.
3. Implement fixes such as caching or asynchronous processing.

Code Example: Profiling Workflow Performance

python

```
import cProfile
```

```python
def workflow():
    for _ in range(1000000):
        pass

cProfile.run("workflow()")
```

29.6 Practice Problems and Quizzes

29.6.1 Mastering Troubleshooting and Optimization Skills

Problem: Optimize the following code to reduce execution time:

python

```
data = [i for i in range(1000000) if i % 2 == 0]
```
Hint: Use efficient list comprehensions or filtering.

29.6.2 Interactive Quizzes

Question: Which tool is best suited for monitoring real-time metrics in an AutoGen system?

1. Prometheus.
2. Jupyter Notebook.
3. Docker.

Answer: 1. Prometheus.

29.7 End-of-Chapter Summaries

29.7.1 Key Takeaways

- Troubleshooting involves structured diagnosis using logs and debugging tools.
- Optimization improves performance and reduces costs through asynchronous processing and resource management.

29.7.2 Quick Reference Guides

Task	Tool	Purpose
Debugging	Python Logging	Analyze and resolve issues.
Performance Profiling	cProfile	Identify workflow bottlenecks.
Monitoring	Grafana	Visualize real-time metrics.

29.8 Templates and Tools

29.8.1 Workflow Templates

Template for Optimizing AutoGen Workflows:

1. Analyze logs to identify issues.
2. Use profiling tools to detect bottlenecks.
3. Implement fixes such as asynchronous processing or caching.

29.8.2 Scripts and Snippets

Reusable Snippet for Logging Errors

python

def divide_numbers(a, b):

```
try:
    return a / b
except ZeroDivisionError as e:
    logging.error(f"Error: {e}")
    return None

print(divide_numbers(10, 0))
```

Mastering troubleshooting and optimization ensures that AutoGen workflows perform efficiently and effectively. By adopting structured debugging practices, leveraging advanced tools, and implementing cost-efficient strategies, users can create resilient and scalable systems.

Chapter 30: Case Study Methodology

Case studies are a powerful tool for understanding, analyzing, and applying real-world applications of AutoGen systems. By documenting successes, challenges, and lessons learned, organizations and individuals can gain actionable insights and refine their strategies for workflow automation. This chapter provides a comprehensive guide to analyzing existing case studies, designing your own, and effectively documenting findings to maximize their value.

30.1 Analyzing and Learning from Case Studies

30.1.1 Frameworks for Effective Case Study Analysis

1. Why Analyze Case Studies?

- Provides practical insights into the implementation of AutoGen systems.
- Identifies strategies and techniques that can be adapted to similar challenges.

2. Key Analysis Frameworks:

- **SWOT Analysis (Strengths, Weaknesses, Opportunities, Threats):**
    - Evaluate the project's internal and external factors.
- **PESTLE Analysis (Political, Economic, Social, Technological, Legal, Environmental):**
    - Understand the macro-environment influencing the project.
- **Root Cause Analysis (RCA):**

- Identify underlying issues that led to challenges or successes.

Example Table: SWOT Analysis for an AutoGen Case Study

Category	Details
Strengths	Reduced processing time by 40%.
Weaknesses	High initial deployment costs.
Opportunities	Expand to adjacent business areas.
Threats	Regulatory changes affecting data usage.

30.1.2 Extracting Lessons and Best Practices

1. Common Areas of Insight:

- **Process Improvements:** Workflow redesigns that enhanced efficiency.
- **Tools and Technologies:** Software that delivered measurable value.
- **Human Factors:** Training and engagement strategies for successful adoption.

2. Techniques for Extracting Lessons:

- **Pattern Recognition:** Identify recurring strategies across multiple case studies.
- **Comparative Analysis:** Compare different implementations to find the most effective approaches.

30.2 Designing Your Own Case Studies

30.2.1 Structuring and Documenting Projects

1. **Key Components of a Case Study:**

    - **Objective:** Define the purpose of the project (e.g., reduce costs, improve efficiency).
    - **Background:** Provide context, including the problem and organizational environment.
    - **Implementation:** Detail the steps taken, including tools and workflows used.
    - **Outcomes:** Highlight measurable results, such as time saved or costs reduced.
    - **Lessons Learned:** Summarize key takeaways.

2. **Example Structure:**

Section	Details
Introduction	Overview of the organization and the challenge addressed.
Solution	Description of the AutoGen system implemented.
Results	Quantifiable benefits and improvements achieved.
Challenges	Issues encountered and how they were resolved.

30.2.2 Presenting Findings and Insights

1. **Presentation Formats:**

    - **Reports:** Detailed written documentation with charts, tables, and narratives.
    - **Presentations:** Use slides to highlight key points visually.
    - **Videos:** Create short clips summarizing the project for easy dissemination.

Example Slide Content for a Case Study Presentation

- Slide 1: Project Overview (Objective, Scope).

- Slide 2: Implementation Details (Tools, Workflow).
- Slide 3: Results (Metrics, ROI).
- Slide 4: Lessons Learned.

30.3 Case Study Documentation Techniques

30.3.1 Effective Reporting and Visualization

1. Essential Visualizations:

- **Before-and-After Charts:** Show the impact of automation.
- **Workflow Diagrams:** Illustrate the processes automated by AutoGen.

Example: Workflow Diagram

text

```
Manual Workflow  -> Automated Workflow
Step 1: Data Entry   -> Automated ETL Process
Step 2: Analysis     -> AI-Driven Insights
Step 3: Reporting    -> AutoGen Report Generator
```

30.3.2 Communicating Successes and Learnings

1. Emphasizing Impact:

- Focus on measurable outcomes such as time saved, errors reduced, or customer satisfaction improvements.
- Include testimonials or feedback from stakeholders.

Example Report Excerpt

text

After implementing the AutoGen-powered inventory management system, the company achieved:

- A 35% reduction in stockouts.
- A 20% improvement in order fulfillment times.
- Over $100,000 saved annually in inventory holding costs.

30.4 Interactive Case Study Exercises

30.4.1 Analyzing Real-World AutoGen Implementations

1. Exercise: Review the following scenario and answer the questions below:

text

A financial services firm implemented an AutoGen system to automate fraud detection. Despite initial success, false positives increased by 25%, frustrating the fraud team.

- Identify the root cause of increased false positives.
- Propose potential solutions.

30.4.2 Developing Your Own Case Studies

1. Exercise: Create a case study for a hypothetical AutoGen implementation in a healthcare setting. Include:

- The problem addressed.
- The tools and workflows implemented.
- The results achieved.

30.5 Hands-On Project

30.5.1 Creating a Comprehensive Case Study of an AutoGen Implementation

Objective: Develop a detailed case study documenting an AutoGen project from start to finish.

Steps:

1. Choose an AutoGen use case (e.g., customer support automation).
2. Collect data on implementation steps, tools, and outcomes.
3. Structure and present findings using charts and visuals.

Example Code: Analyzing Performance Data for Case Studies

python

```
import pandas as pd
import matplotlib.pyplot as plt

# Sample performance data
data = pd.DataFrame({
    "Month": ["January", "February", "March"],
    "Manual Process Time (hrs)": [500, 450, 400],
    "AutoGen Process Time (hrs)": [300, 250, 200]
})

# Visualization
plt.plot(data["Month"], data["Manual Process Time (hrs)"], label="Manual")
plt.plot(data["Month"], data["AutoGen Process Time (hrs)"], label="AutoGen")
plt.xlabel("Month")
```

```
plt.ylabel("Processing Time (hrs)")
plt.title("Performance Improvement")
plt.legend()
plt.show()
```

30.6 Practice Problems and Quizzes

30.6.1 Enhancing Analytical Skills through Case Study Analysis

Problem: Analyze the following metrics from an AutoGen implementation and determine areas for improvement:

- Task Completion Time: Reduced by 20%.
- Error Rate: Increased by 15%.

30.6.2 Interactive Quizzes

Question: Which section of a case study focuses on quantifiable outcomes?

1. Objective.
2. Implementation.
3. Results.

Answer: 3. Results.

30.7 End-of-Chapter Summaries

30.7.1 Key Takeaways

- Case studies provide actionable insights by documenting real-world implementations.

- Effective reporting and visualization enhance the communication of findings.

30.7.2 Quick Reference Guides

Task	Tool	Purpose
Analyzing Case Studies	SWOT, PESTLE	Frameworks for structured analysis.
Visualizing Outcomes	Matplotlib, Tableau	Create impactful visualizations.

30.8 Templates and Tools

30.8.1 Workflow Templates

Template for Case Study Analysis:

1. Define the objective and scope.
2. Gather and document data on implementation.
3. Analyze results and identify lessons learned.

30.8.2 Scripts and Snippets

Reusable Snippet for Data Comparison

python

```python
def compare_metrics(before, after):
    improvement = ((before - after) / before) * 100
    return f"Improvement: {improvement:.2f}%"

# Example usage
print(compare_metrics(500, 300))
```

Case studies are invaluable for understanding the nuances of AutoGen implementations. By analyzing, designing, and documenting them effectively, practitioners can extract lessons, share insights, and contribute to the growth of the AutoGen ecosystem.

Chapter 31: Feedback Mechanisms and Continuous Improvement

Feedback mechanisms are essential for refining processes, improving content, and fostering innovation in any field. In the context of AutoGen workflows and this book, gathering feedback ensures relevance, accuracy, and alignment with the needs of the community. This chapter discusses how to set up feedback systems, utilize input effectively, and create an iterative improvement loop.

31.1 Encouraging Reader Feedback

31.1.1 Setting Up Feedback Channels

1. Importance of Feedback:

- Validates the effectiveness of workflows and content.
- Highlights areas for improvement or expansion.
- Enhances user engagement and trust.

2. Effective Feedback Channels:

- **Online Surveys:** Use platforms like Google Forms or Typeform for structured feedback.
- **Email Feedback:** Provide a dedicated email address for suggestions and queries.
- **Community Forums:** Engage in discussions on platforms like Reddit, Discord, or Slack.

Example Feedback Form Questions:

1. Was the content easy to understand?
2. Which sections were the most helpful?
3. What improvements would you suggest for future editions?

Code Example: Automating Feedback Collection

python

```
import smtplib
from email.mime.text import MIMEText

def send_feedback_email(email, message):
    smtp = smtplib.SMTP("smtp.example.com", 587)
    smtp.starttls()
    smtp.login("your_email@example.com", "your_password")
    msg = MIMEText(message)
    msg["Subject"] = "Feedback Request"
    msg["From"] = "your_email@example.com"
    msg["To"] = email
    smtp.sendmail("your_email@example.com", email, msg.as_string())
    smtp.quit()

# Example usage
send_feedback_email("reader@example.com", "We value your feedback. Please reply with your thoughts!")
```

31.1.2 Utilizing Feedback for Content Refinement

1. Categorizing Feedback:

- **Actionable:** Specific suggestions or corrections.
- **General:** Broader comments or preferences.
- **Positive:** Areas of success to retain and build upon.

2. Processing Feedback:

- Use tools like Trello or Jira to manage and prioritize feedback.
- Organize input into themes for targeted improvements.

Example Table: Categorizing Feedback

Feedback Type	Example	Action
Actionable	"Add more code examples for Chapter 5."	Include additional examples.
General	"Expand on best practices for debugging."	Extend relevant sections.
Positive	"The case studies were very insightful."	Highlight similar content in future.

31.2 Iterative Content Development

31.2.1 Incorporating Feedback into Future Editions

1. Steps to Incorporate Feedback:

- Regularly review feedback from surveys and emails.
- Assess feasibility and relevance of suggestions.
- Schedule updates or errata for future editions.

2. Examples of Iterative Improvements:

- Adding a new chapter based on popular demand.
- Refining examples or templates to address confusion.

Code Example: Version Tracking for Updates

python

```python
class ContentVersion:
    def __init__(self, version, changes):
        self.version = version
        self.changes = changes
```

```
    def display_changes(self):
        print(f"Version: {self.version}")
        for change in self.changes:
            print(f"- {change}")

# Example usage
update = ContentVersion("2.0", ["Added new case studies", "Refined Chapter 10 examples"])
update.display_changes()
```

31.2.2 Best Practices for Continuous Improvement

1. Establish a Feedback Cycle:

- Gather input during and after releases.
- Communicate changes back to readers to demonstrate responsiveness.

2. Maintain a Change Log:

- Keep a transparent record of updates for readers.

Example Change Log Structure:

Version	Changes	Date
1.1	Added templates in Chapter 8.	Jan 2024
1.2	Corrected errors in Chapter 12 code examples.	Mar 2024

31.3 Building a Feedback Loop with the Community

31.3.1 Engaging Readers for Ongoing Contributions

1. Fostering Engagement:

- Encourage readers to suggest improvements or share their experiences.
- Recognize contributors in future editions or online platforms.

2. Example Community Initiatives:

- Host webinars or live Q&A sessions.
- Create a GitHub repository for collaborative projects.

31.3.2 Leveraging Community Insights for Enhancement

1. Tapping into Collective Knowledge:

- Use forums and discussion groups to gain diverse perspectives.
- Collaborate with experts to refine workflows or methodologies.

Example: Using a Community Poll

python

```python
from matplotlib import pyplot as plt

# Poll results
feedback_types = ["More Examples", "New Topics", "Interactive Tools"]
votes = [50, 30, 20]

# Plot poll results
plt.bar(feedback_types, votes)
plt.title("Reader Feedback Poll Results")
plt.ylabel("Votes")
plt.show()
```

31.4 Hands-On Project

31.4.1 Creating a Feedback System for Your AutoGen Workflows

Objective: Develop an automated feedback system for users of an AutoGen workflow.

Steps:

1. Set up a feedback collection form using Google Forms or a web app.
2. Integrate responses into a database for analysis.
3. Generate summary reports to highlight trends.

31.5 Practice Problems and Quizzes

31.5.1 Implementing Effective Feedback Mechanisms

Problem: Design a feedback mechanism for a newly deployed AutoGen system. Identify key questions to ask and the tools you would use.

31.5.2 Interactive Quizzes

Question: What is the primary benefit of a feedback loop in AutoGen workflows?

1. Faster system performance.
2. Continuous improvement.
3. Increased automation speed.

Answer: 2. Continuous improvement.

31.6 End-of-Chapter Summaries

31.6.1 Key Takeaways

- Feedback mechanisms enhance AutoGen systems by addressing user needs.
- Continuous improvement relies on structured feedback loops and iterative development.

31.6.2 Quick Reference Guides

Task	Tool	Purpose
Collecting Feedback	Google Forms, Slack	Gather user insights.
Managing Feedback	Trello, Jira	Organize and prioritize input.

31.7 Templates and Tools

31.7.1 Workflow Templates

Template for Feedback Integration:

1. Collect feedback using forms or surveys.
2. Categorize input into actionable themes.
3. Schedule regular reviews and updates.

31.7.2 Scripts and Snippets

Reusable Snippet for Feedback Categorization

python

```
def categorize_feedback(feedback):
```

```python
    if "example" in feedback.lower():
        return "Actionable"
    elif "general" in feedback.lower():
        return "General"
    else:
        return "Positive"

# Example usage
feedback = "Add more examples in Chapter 5."
print(categorize_feedback(feedback))
```

Feedback is the cornerstone of continuous improvement. By establishing robust mechanisms, engaging with the community, and iteratively refining content and workflows, AutoGen practitioners and authors can stay relevant and responsive to evolving needs.

Appendix A: Glossary of Key Terms

This appendix provides a comprehensive glossary of key terms and concepts used throughout the book. Each definition is concise and designed to provide clarity for both beginners and experienced readers.

Term	Definition
AutoGen	A framework or methodology that automates workflows using generative AI and machine learning.
Generative AI	AI systems that create new content, such as text, images, or code, based on input data.
Workflow Automation	The use of technology to perform repetitive tasks without human intervention.
LLM (Large Language Model)	A type of AI model trained on vast amounts of text data to understand and generate human-like language.
ETL (Extract, Transform, Load)	A process for extracting data from sources, transforming it into usable formats, and loading it into a system.
Knowledge Graph	A structured representation of data that connects entities and their relationships.
RESTful API	An application programming interface that follows REST principles, enabling smooth data exchange.
Case Study	An in-depth analysis of a real-world implementation to extract lessons and insights.

Appendix B: Additional Resources and References

This appendix lists additional resources to deepen your understanding of AutoGen and related topics. Explore these materials for further reading, learning, and implementation.

B.1 Recommended Books, Articles, and Research Papers

Books:

1. *Deep Learning* by Ian Goodfellow et al.
2. *AI Superpowers* by Kai-Fu Lee.
3. *Designing Data-Intensive Applications* by Martin Kleppmann.

Articles:

- "The Future of Generative AI" – Harvard Business Review.
- "Workflow Automation in the Age of AI" – IEEE Spectrum.

Research Papers:

- Brown et al., "Language Models are Few-Shot Learners," NeurIPS, 2020.
- Bengio et al., "Deep Learning for Workflow Automation," Journal of AI Research, 2021.

B.2 Online Courses and Tutorials

1. **Coursera:**
    - *AI for Everyone* by Andrew Ng.
    - *Generative Adversarial Networks (GANs)* by DeepLearning.AI.

2. **Udemy:**
   - *Mastering Workflow Automation with Python.*
   - *Introduction to AutoGen Frameworks.*
3. **YouTube Channels:**
   - *StatQuest with Josh Starmer* (explains AI and ML concepts).
   - *TechWithTim* (programming tutorials, including workflow automation).

B.3 Useful Tools and Libraries for AutoGen

Tool/Library	Purpose
LangChain	Building applications with LLMs.
Airflow	Workflow orchestration and scheduling.
DALL-E	Generative AI for image creation.
PyTorch	Deep learning framework for model training.
TensorFlow	AI framework for building and training models.

B.4 Industry Reports and Whitepapers

1. *AI in Workflow Automation: Trends and Predictions* – McKinsey & Company.
2. *Generative AI for Enterprise Applications* – Gartner Research.
3. *The Future of Automation in Key Industries* – Forrester.

Appendix C: Sample AutoGen Workflows and Templates

This appendix provides pre-designed workflow templates and example configurations to help you get started with AutoGen in various domains.

C.1 Pre-Designed Workflow Templates for Common Use Cases

Example: Email Campaign Automation Workflow

1. Collect email addresses from a database.
2. Generate personalized email content using an LLM.
3. Schedule and send emails via an API.

python

```
from emailer import EmailSender
from llm import TextGenerator

emails = ["user1@example.com", "user2@example.com"]
for email in emails:
    content = TextGenerator.generate_personalized_email(email)
    EmailSender.send_email(email, content)
```

C.2 Example Configurations for Different Industries

Healthcare:

- Automating patient appointment scheduling with AI.

Finance:

- Automating financial report generation with workflow tools.

Retail:

- Inventory management using predictive analytics.

C.3 Downloadable Templates and Scripts

Access ready-to-use templates and scripts for:

- ETL processes.
- Workflow orchestration.
- Dashboard creation.

Appendix D: Troubleshooting and FAQs

This appendix addresses common challenges and questions to help you troubleshoot and resolve issues quickly.

D.1 Common Issues and Their Solutions

Issue: Slow AutoGen workflow execution.

- **Solution:** Optimize database queries, use asynchronous processing, and enable caching.

Issue: Errors in data pipelines.

- **Solution:** Validate input data formats and ensure proper ETL configurations.

D.2 Frequently Asked Questions About AutoGen

Q: What industries can benefit most from AutoGen? **A:** AutoGen is widely applicable across industries like healthcare, finance, e-commerce, and education.

Q: Do I need programming skills to use AutoGen? **A:** While basic programming knowledge is helpful, many tools offer low-code or no-code interfaces.

D.3 Additional Troubleshooting Tips

1. Use structured logging for easier debugging.
2. Leverage monitoring tools like Prometheus for real-time metrics.

Appendix E: Contributor Bios

This appendix features profiles of the experts and contributors who have enriched this book with their insights and expertise.

Name	Expertise	Contribution
Dr. Jane Doe	AI and Machine Learning	Provided insights on generative AI frameworks.
John Smith	Workflow Automation Specialist	Designed case studies and example workflows.
Alice Johnson	Data Scientist	Authored sections on data analysis techniques.

These appendices are designed to be a practical reference for further learning and exploration. Whether you are troubleshooting issues, exploring additional resources, or learning from real-world workflows, these tools will guide your journey in mastering AutoGen.

Index

This comprehensive index provides an alphabetical listing of topics, terms, and concepts covered in the book. Use it as a quick reference to locate specific sections, definitions, and examples within the text.

A

- Adaptive Learning Systems: Chapter 13
- Advanced Debugging Techniques: Chapter 29
- AI and Digital Transformation: Chapter 26
- AI Assistants in Education: Chapter 13
- AI Governance and Policy: Chapter 27
- AI-Driven Content Tools: Chapter 24
- AutoGen Case Study Methodology: Chapter 30
- AutoGen Glossary: Appendix A
- AutoGen Implementation Challenges: Chapter 29
- AutoGen in Education: Chapter 23
- AutoGen in E-commerce: Chapter 22
- AutoGen in Finance: Chapter 21
- AutoGen in Healthcare: Chapter 20
- Automating Campaign Management: Chapter 24
- Automating Diagnostic Processes: Chapter 20
- Automating Financial Reporting: Chapter 21
- Automating Knowledge Graphs: Chapter 12
- Automating Patient Data Management: Chapter 20
- Automating Supply Chain Processes: Chapter 22

- Automated Incident Response: Chapter 18
- Automated Workflow Templates: Appendix C

B

- Best Practices in Workflow Automation: Chapters 2, 16
- Blockchain and AutoGen: Chapter 15
- Budgeting for AutoGen Systems: Chapter 16
- Building Community Engagement: Chapter 28
- Building Knowledge Repositories: Chapter 12

C

- Case Studies in Workflow Automation: Chapter 30
- Caching Strategies: Chapters 16, 29
- Cloud-Based Automation: Chapter 16
- Community Support for AutoGen: Chapter 28
- Compliance Monitoring: Chapter 17
- Content Generation with AutoGen: Chapter 5
- Cost Optimization Strategies: Chapter 16
- Cross-Platform Integration: Chapters 15, 19
- Customizing Large Language Models: Chapter 19

D

- Data Analytics in AutoGen: Chapter 9
- Data Cleaning Techniques: Chapter 9
- Decision Support Systems: Chapter 11

- Designing Educational Workflows: Chapter 23
- Designing Multi-Agent Systems: Chapter 7
- Distributed Workflow Automation: Chapter 15

E

- Education Automation with AutoGen: Chapter 23
- Emerging Trends in Automation: Chapter 26
- End-of-Chapter Summaries: All Chapters
- Ethical Considerations in AI: Chapter 4
- ETL Processes: Chapters 3, 9

F

- Fraud Detection with AutoGen: Chapter 21
- Feedback Mechanisms: Chapter 31
- Fine-Tuning AI Models: Chapter 19
- Financial Modeling Automation: Chapter 11
- Frameworks for AutoGen: Chapter 3

H

- Hands-On Projects: All Chapters
- Healthcare Analytics: Chapter 20
- Human-AI Collaboration: Chapter 26

I

- Interactive Dashboards: Chapter 9

- Interactive Quizzes: All Chapters
- Internet of Things (IoT) and AutoGen: Chapter 15

K

- Knowledge Management Automation: Chapter 12
- Knowledge Graph Tools: Chapter 12

L

- Large Language Models (LLMs): Chapter 3
- Leveraging Feedback Loops: Chapter 31
- Logging and Monitoring Tools: Chapter 18

M

- Multi-Agent Coordination Strategies: Chapter 7
- Multi-Modal AI Innovations: Chapter 26

N

- Natural Language Understanding (NLU): Chapter 8

O

- Observability in AutoGen Systems: Chapter 18
- Online Tutorials and Courses: Appendix B
- Optimization Techniques: Chapter 16
- Overcoming Automation Challenges: Chapter 29

P

- Patient Data Management: Chapter 20
- Performance Tuning: Chapter 16
- Personalized Education Automation: Chapter 13
- Predictive Maintenance in Manufacturing: Chapter 25
- Privacy and Security in AutoGen: Chapter 17

R

- Reporting and Visualization: Chapter 9, Appendix C
- RESTful APIs in Automation: Chapter 3
- Risk Management with AI: Chapter 21

S

- Scaling AutoGen Systems: Chapter 16
- Scenario Analysis Automation: Chapter 11
- Security Best Practices: Chapter 17
- Simulation and Prototyping Tools: Chapter 14
- Supply Chain Automation: Chapters 22, 25
- Sustainable AI Practices: Chapter 4

T

- Templates and Tools: All Chapters, Appendices C & D
- Troubleshooting Techniques: Chapter 29

V

- Visualization Tools: Chapters 9, 18

W

- Workflow Automation Case Studies: Chapter 30
- Workflow Design Best Practices: Chapter 7
- Workflow Templates: Appendix C

Z

- Zero Downtime Workflow Optimization: Chapter 16

This index ensures that readers can quickly locate the information they need to master the art and science of AutoGen workflows

Conclusion

Congratulations on completing This Book! By making it this far, you've embarked on a transformative journey to unlock the immense power of AI-driven automation. From foundational principles to advanced techniques and real-world applications, you now possess the tools, knowledge, and confidence to implement AutoGen systems that drive efficiency, innovation, and growth.

This book was designed to be more than just a one-time read – it is a **living resource** for you to return to again and again as you expand your skills. Whether you are an AI enthusiast, developer, business leader, or innovator, the practical projects, templates, and hands-on examples ensure that *Mastering AutoGen* remains a trusted companion on your automation journey.

Why Revisit This Book?

1. **Deeper Learning with Practice**: Many chapters include hands-on projects, case studies, and practice problems. Revisit them to refine your skills, explore advanced concepts, or try new approaches to solving problems. Every return unlocks another layer of learning.

2. **Stay Relevant**: As AutoGen technologies evolve, so will your understanding. Use the book's foundational knowledge as a springboard for exploring future trends and innovations discussed in the later chapters.

3. **Use It as a Reference**: Need a quick workflow template? A troubleshooting solution? A refresher on API integration? The structured chapters and appendices are built for easy navigation, so you can find what you need quickly.

Your Voice Matters

If you found this book valuable, your feedback is essential. Share your thoughts, experiences, and insights by leaving a review. Your review not only helps others discover this book but also allows me to improve future editions and expand the AutoGen community.

Share the Knowledge

True learning happens when knowledge is shared. Talk about the projects you've completed, the workflows you've automated, and the insights you've gained. Recommend this book to your peers, colleagues, and networks. Share what you've built – whether it's a personalized learning platform, an AI-powered chatbot, or a predictive analytics system – and inspire others to explore the possibilities of AutoGen.

Join the Community

The journey doesn't stop here. Engage with the growing AutoGen community, whether through forums, online discussions, or collaborative projects. Connect with fellow readers and practitioners to exchange ideas, troubleshoot challenges, and push the boundaries of what's possible with workflow automation.

The Future Awaits

As you step forward into the world of AI-driven automation, remember this: you are not just adopting a technology; you are shaping the future. AutoGen is a powerful tool, but its full potential lies in your hands – in your creativity, vision, and ambition to solve real-world challenges. Use what you've learned here to build smarter systems, unlock new efficiencies, and make a meaningful impact in your field.

Follow me on Amazon so you can be notified anytime I drop a new body of work.

Thank you for being part of this journey. Let this be just the beginning of your mastery of AutoGen.

www.ingramcontent.com/pod-product-compliance
Lightning Source LLC
Chambersburg PA
CBHW062100220526
45471CB00010B/3547